BLINDSIGHT
AND THE NATURE OF
CONSCIOUSNESS

BLINDSIGHT
AND THE NATURE OF
CONSCIOUSNESS

JASON HOLT

broadview press

National Library of Canada Cataloguing in Publication

Holt, Jason, 1971-
Blindsight and the nature of consciousness / Jason Holt.
Includes bibliographical references.

ISBN 1-55111-351-1

1. Visual perception—Philosophy. 2. Consciousness. I. Title.

BF311.H65 2003   126   C2002-904608-4

Broadview Press Ltd. is an independent, international publishing house, incorporated in 1985. Broadview believes in shared ownership, both with its employees and with the general public; since the year 2000 Broadview shares have traded publicly on the Toronto Venture Exchange under the symbol BDP.

We welcome comments and suggestions regarding any aspect of our publications—please feel free to contact us at the addresses below or at broadview@broadviewpress.com.

North America
PO Box 1243, Peterborough, Ontario, Canada K9J 7H5
3576 California Road, Orchard Park, NY, USA 14127
Tel: (705) 743-8990; Fax: (705) 743-8353
email: customerservice@broadviewpress.com

UK, Ireland, and continental Europe
Thomas Lyster Ltd., Units 3 & 4a, Old Boundary Way
Burscough Road, Ormskirk
Lancashire, L39 2YW
Tel: (01695) 575112; Fax: (01695) 570120
email: books@tlyster.co.uk

Australia and New Zealand
UNIREPS, University of New South Wales
Sydney, NSW, 2052
Tel: 61 2 9664 0999; Fax: 61 2 9664 5420
email: info.press@unsw.edu.au

www.broadviewpress.com

Broadview Press Ltd. gratefully acknowledges the financial support of the Government of Canada through the Book Publishing Industry Development Program for our publishing activities.

 This book is printed on acid-free paper containing 30% post-consumer fibre.

CONTENTS

T HIS BOOK IS ABOUT CONSCIOUSNESS and a phenomenon that conspicuously lacks it. The phenomenon is blindsight, one of the most controversial and important scientific discoveries in recent decades. Blindsight is the surprising ability of people with a certain kind of brain damage to perceive things visually even though they lack visual experience completely.[1] They "see" without *seeing*. The word itself sounds like an oxymoron, and yet it is quite apt, not despite this fact, but rather because of it. For the lack of visual consciousness, it is blind, and for the ability of the visual system, so handicapped, to take in and deploy information about the world, it is a kind of sight. People with blindsight are unaware of the information they possess, even when they use it, and so their judgments seem to them haphazard, mere guesswork. But their judgments are too reliable for this to be the case. It is not mere guesswork. It *cannot* be. Their shots in the dark betray excellent marksmanship.

This is all very interesting, perhaps, but why write a book about it? There are a number of reasons, actually. The notion that one can "see" without *seeing* may strike one as odd, if not absurd. The phenomenon itself is intriguing, and more than passing reference to it can be found in works of both high and popular culture, including novels, plays, television programs, music, and books of wide appeal despite their technical orientation. Trying to explain blindsight is no less challenging. Early experiments sparked heated debates in the psychology literature, some of which are still ongoing. Philosophers were among the first to be intrigued. They began discussing blindsight in the late 1970s, almost a decade before the first detailed case-study was published.[2] The phenomenon has since gained much greater currency, to the point where it is now standard issue subject matter not only in psychology and the neurosciences, but in philosophy of mind. Indeed, blindsight is at the forefront of a new wave of scientific studies and philosophical investigations of consciousness. It promises to help us discover important facts about not only the functional architecture of the brain, but also the neurological basis and—perhaps—even the true nature of consciousness.

I first became interested in blindsight while doing graduate work at the University of Western Ontario.[3] I was not surprised that philosophers were discussing blindsight, nor that they seemed to attach such importance to it that it made a well-known list of the top ten problems of consciousness.[4] Nor was I surprised that a number of clever arguments, based on blindsight, had been constructed to support a wide variety of philosophical views. The phenomenon itself is something of a shocker, so it is only natural to expect that it has telling, if not shocking, implications. The way most of us think about the mind is fine for practical purposes. However, common sense does not anticipate such phenomena as blindsight, and, since a refined understanding of the mind will be sensitive to such phenomena, common sense will have to give way at some point, although where it will have to give way is not altogether clear. There are huge differences of opinion as to what blindsight implies about the nature of consciousness. The surprising thing is that there has been little effort to settle these disputes. In fact, despite the perceived importance of blindsight, there has been *no* extended treatment of it from a philosophical perspective.

It was with an eye to filling this gap that I wrote my doctoral thesis on blindsight and its philosophical applications. It is from that thesis that this little book has been cultivated. There has been some new growth since then, as well as some pruning. Up till now, philosophers have discussed blindsight primarily in connection with consciousness. This is not surprising; the connection is obvious. What is odd, I think, is that philosophers have discussed blindsight almost *exclusively* in connection with consciousness. Other areas of philosophical concern, theories of knowledge and perception in particular, on which blindsight is likely to bear, have been largely ignored. Much of the new growth I speak of lies in exploring such neglected applications. As for the pruning, some of the drier, more technical bits of the thesis have been relegated to endnotes or else omitted entirely. My intent is to maintain enough conceptual rigour to satisfy those of my ilk, while presenting a book that is accessible to non-philosophers—including specialists in psychology, the neurosciences, and other cognate disciplines—as well as students and non-academics interested in the subject.

That said, I want to take the rest of this introduction to paint a backdrop against which an encounter with blindsight will stand in appropriate relief. The backdrop, suitably enough, looms large. It is the problem of consciousness. Beginning here, we will eventually come to see how something so rare and peculiar as blindsight can illuminate something so commonplace as consciousness. If you do not need a crash-course in the mind/body problem, and you do not want a refresher, feel free to skip ahead.

Consciousness is exotic. It is also mundane. Funny that. Consider, right now, the panoply of your present experiences, of the world around you, the things in it, your place among them, your body's orientation, various thoughts, various feelings. Now recall some past event. Imagine a scenario. Form an intention. Act on it. Infer something trivial about the author of this book. Note the colour of the book's cover, the thickness, the texture, the sound of pages flipped under your thumb. Focus your attention on each word in this sentence, the shape of the letters, the style of font. Mark your sense of the passage of time, your sense of self, of how it all seems to come together in each moment and flow smoothly, coherently to the next. So much awareness!—and all the waking live-long day. Such is the mundanity of consciousness. It almost goes without saying. But that is *your* consciousness. To others your consciousness is something exotic, closed off, available at best to imperfect imagination and felicitous inference. Why, then, is it so unavoidably easy to think of others as conscious? Part of the reason is that others behave with intelligence and cognizance more or less as you do, and you know—or think you know—that in your own case consciousness helps produce such actions. Without evidence that you are an anomaly, a lone consciousness in a sea of biological automata, the only sane default is that other *homines sapientes* are conscious, just like you. The evidence for commonality, here, outweighs that for anomaly by an appreciable margin.

Although exotic in one sense, other people's consciousness is, practically speaking, mundane. We are a sentient species. We should be able to account for this fact scientifically, if, that is, science offers the sort of "theory of everything" we think it does. But consciousness seems especially exotic to worldviews that would have everything in the universe accounted for by the physical and biological sciences. The progress of these sciences is so rapid, the achievements so comprehensively impressive, that there appears little need for consciousness and even less room for it. Even in those sciences aimed at modelling the human mind, most theories get on fine without considering consciousness and fail to catch it besides. Building such models does not have to involve much consideration of where consciousness fits in the overall scheme of things. Such consideration seems anathema to machine-building and response-measuring, even where the machines are meant to model sentience and even where the responses measured are those of conscious human subjects. Cognitive flowcharts omitting consciousness do not seem incomplete, and those including it appear suspect. Yet consciousness remains irreplaceably our vantage on ourselves and the world around us, without which it would be impossible to have the very sciences that seem to threaten it. Despite much renewed interest in the scientific study of consciousness, the old habits die hard, and no one knows exactly what new procedures should replace them.

From a certain point of view, it seems that consciousness cannot be *both* exotic and mundane. One of these two perspectives must be privileged, the other dismissed. Tough-minded souls may say—some have—"So much the worse for consciousness!" By the same token, tender-minded friends of the ethereal, poets and the like, may counter with equal conviction, if not cachet, "So much the worse for science!" Here is a more diplomatic suggestion: "Let scientists speak of quarks and biological imperatives and computational processes—and nothing besides—and let ordinary folk speak of consciousness." Unfortunately, such diplomatic suggestions are based on a misunderstanding of the scope of science and the limits of common sense. They do not resolve the tension, they *dissolve* it. Dissolving the tension, in this case, amounts to failing to appreciate just what a problem the problem of consciousness is.

To more fully appreciate the tension between the exotic and the mundane in consciousness, we will take a budget tour of the mind/body problem from inception to present day, a history representing a clear, linear progression of thought. The plateaux in this progression reveal whence sprang the current philosophical landscape. They also continue to shape debate, sometimes incognito. As such, our budget tour will be doubly instructive. What gets the ball rolling is the idea, innocent enough, that mind is fundamentally different from matter. What keeps it rolling is inertia.

Our story begins, as does modern philosophy itself, with Descartes, whose famous dictum *I think, therefore I am* encapsulates a worldview so profoundly influential that, to this day, it suffuses our culture. Just think of the catchphrase "mind over matter" if you do not believe me. For Descartes, the thing of which one can be most certain is that one exists, a thinker of thoughts, a subject of experience. One is *essentially* a mind, and while the essence of mind is thought, the essence of coffee cups and continents and all things material is shape. Material objects have dimension. They are extended in space, subject to physical and mechanical laws that have no purchase in the mind's domain. It is within this basic worldview that the mind/body problem emerges, salient and profound. When I see my coffee cup and, wanting a swig of coffee, reach for it, mind and matter appear to interact. My visual experience is caused by the cup, and my intention to drink causes me to reach for it. This is unremarkable. But how, according to Descartes, do mind and matter interact when they differ so fundamentally in essence and governance? They just do. Where does this causal interaction take place? At the pineal gland, Descartes thought, a symmetrical and relatively central structure in the brain. This hypothesis is, as a matter of fact, false. But it is a minor hypothesis. Descartes' error has nothing to do with the pineal gland. The fault lies, instead, in his conception of the mind as a sort of ghost haunting our corporeal machinery.

The account of mind/body interaction offered by Descartes is an explanation *ad mysterium*, and such appeals to mystery are notoriously weak. Behaviourists diagnose the problem as one of categorization. On this view, Descartes errs by thinking that the mind is something substantial, that it has a *je ne sais quoi* over and above what is revealed, at least potentially, in action. Just as, in sports, there is no "team spirit" apart from the vigorous play of players, their cheering each other on, locker-room camaraderie, and so on, so too there is no "mind spirit" apart from what the body does and how it does it.[5] It is the machine that matters, not the ghost, and so the ghost evaporates like the myth it is, as ghosts are wont to do. Supposing otherwise is not substance dualism, it is substance *abuse*, a miscategorization of mind. My pain is not independent of the behaviour that reveals it to others. Indeed, if the mind were a spiritual substance, it would be insulated from such revelation, and we would have a devil of a time trying to discern other people's mental states. But often enough we do not have a difficult time discerning what is on someone's mind. Your smile indicates happiness, my gritted teeth frustration. One does not always say "Ouch!"—or the like—when one is in pain, but in such cases, one is still *disposed* to exhibit pain behaviour. Without some such disposition, however weak and to whatever actions it inclines, it would be doubtful that the mental state in question is pain at all. Behaviourism thus identifies mental states not with actual pieces of behaviour but with dispositions to act in mentally transparent ways.

One of the chief flaws of behaviourism is that it conflates the evidence we have for mentality with mentality itself. Actions and their associated dispositions constitute evidence for mental states, and such evidence must not be confused with the things they evince. Trains of thought and other mental processes are seemingly more than a flux of behavioural dispositions. There is something *going on* in a train of thought irrespective of the actions to which each thought may give rise. When someone says "Ouch!" sincerely, it is because they are in pain, but explaining this by citing the disposition to say "Ouch!" does not help. Just as the fragility of glass, its disposition to break easily, requires further explanation, so too does the disposition to say "Ouch!" even where that disposition is identified with pain, which explains, from a commonsense point of view, why "Ouch!" is said.[6] Glass is fragile because of its microphysical properties; small-scale structure explains the disposition. Likewise, from a physical point of view, when one is disposed to say "Ouch!" it is because of the microphysical properties of one's brain. This may seem at odds with common sense, which already provides a perfectly good account of such dispositions in the simple hypothesis, say, that the subject is in pain. But these explanations are not competitors, they are complements. We can avoid scotching either science or common sense by interpreting them as giving different descriptions of the same thing. That is, we identify mental states with those brain states that cause mentally indicative behaviour. I say "Ouch!" because I am in pain and because my brain is in a certain state; that is, my pain simply *is* that brain state. Materialism is the view, simply put, that mental states are brain states. To the mind untempted by Cartesian dualism, this may seem obvious. Thus does philosophy by careful meandering come at last to what should be common sense.

Materialism has its own pitfalls, even setting aside the understandable but mistaken idea that it either involves, or is, a degradation of our species. "Materializing" the mind seems to take personal identity, human freedom, moral character, high art, romantic love, existential angst, and all the wonders of being human and toss them out the window, baby-with-bathwater style. However, in whatever terms we make sense of the mind, most of such talk can be preserved, if reinterpreted. The real problem with materialism is this: it requires that every type of mental state correspond to, and be identical with, one and only one type of physical state. But brains vary significantly over time, across individuals, and across species. It is too unlikely that every instance of pain will correspond with the exact same type of physical state.[7] Even if we discovered such one-to-one mappings across all known species, we might later discover a species that registers pain quite differently. And even if we found that pain had a single, univocal realization in all natural species, we would still have a problem. There is a distinct possibility that we might create, in the not-too-distant future, an autonomous, sentient robot. This may seem a bit far-fetched, but it is not. We are already developing the technology to replace damaged neuronal groups with silicon processors. If someone lost the ability to feel pain, the dysfunction could, in principle, be compensated for by a silicon "painmaker," just as pacemakers and artificial hearts compensate for dysfunctional hearts. Mental states, then, do not correspond to a single physical type, but to a plurality of such types. This means that they are identical, not to any one of their physical realizers, but to the function they all serve. From this perspective, a mental state is simply whatever does the job. This, in a nutshell, is functionalism.

For a while now, the view that mental states are multiply realizable has been all but unquestioned. What to do with this picture is another matter, for functionalism itself seems inadequate. What hamstrings functionalism is its inherent inability to capture the intrinsic nature of consciousness. We can imagine inversion cases, where, for instance, I see red instead of green, yellow instead of blue, and vice versa, without this making any sort of functional difference.[8] You and I agree on the meaning of colour terms and how to apply them, and in every other way when it comes to colour, but my experiences are, if you can imagine this, the opposite of yours, systematically inverted. Our functional states are the same, but our conscious states are not, which means there is something more to consciousness than can be captured in a description of what consciousness does. Unlike brain states, functional states have no intrinsic properties to which raw red experience can be tied. The upshot of this is the somewhat resigned view that mental state types like pain simply cannot be anchored to the natural world in the way we should ideally want. Although the headache I am having right now is to be identified with a particular state of my brain, nothing about its *being a pain* matters to what goes on in the world. Pain *per se* does not show up in the natural order. This motivates the unfortunate claim that science should ignore, and perhaps even deny, the existence of mind. Such is the dilemma of the present state of the art.

The problem of consciousness is not the problem of how human beings can use their appreciable grey matter to reason, acquire knowledge of the world, or behave with intelligence and skill. The problem is rather to explain how so much electrochemical stuff is responsible for what seems most utterly alien to it—the private, subjective, seemingly non-physical stuff of one's own experience, the mind as "seen by itself." How does the machine make the ghost? And what is the ghost made of? This, the problem of sentience, stands in sharp contrast to those of sapience, intelligence, and other conundra of mind, on which considerable advance has been made through the joint efforts of psychologists and philosophers. Consciousness seems effortlessly immune to the attacks of theoretical acumen and inspired speculation that crumble other problems. It is a tough nut to crack, perhaps the toughest. A satisfactory theory of consciousness might require conceptual revision and metaphysical rejigging of a radical kind. Instead of starting with the material world and trying to fit consciousness into it, perhaps we have to assume that there is no matter as such, only minds with impressions out of which the idea of matter is built. Or perhaps the ultimate stuff of the universe is neither mind nor matter but information or some other neutral substance, different aspects of which are mind and matter, or out of which both can be, as it were, "logically constructed." If we cannot find room for consciousness in the material world, these options are not as wild as they seem.

Maybe we *can* find room for consciousness in the material world. It is not yet clear that we cannot, and so metaphysical revision is, at this point, premature, not to mention extreme. At the other extreme is the view that there is no problem of consciousness. A subject's conscious states are simply features of that subject's brain. Nothing more need be said, except by scientists, whose task is to discover what those features are. The appropriate stance, I suggest, is somewhere in between. While consciousness poses no special *metaphysical* problem, of the sort that mandates changing our fundamental view of the universe, it does pose a uniquely significant *conceptual* problem, which is to understand how consciousness could arise from some natural, scientifically determinable feature of the brain.

Having said something about the stance I will take in this book, I should mention other, more pessimistic views on whether consciousness can be captured in naturalist terms.[9] The first is anti-naturalism, according to which consciousness is not natural and, hence, cannot be given a successful naturalist treatment. Consciousness resides in a Cartesian spirit or some other kind of immaterial stuff. Perhaps there is causal interaction between this other substance and the brain, as Descartes thought. Or perhaps there only *appears* to be such interaction because a divine force set it up that way at the beginning of time, the two realms running in harmonious parallel. On the other hand, perhaps the divine force did not set it up that way, occasioning instead the right bodily movements every time someone has an intention and perceptual experiences apropos of the environment. Such views are passé, but this, by itself, is no mark against them. Though most are explanations *ad mysterium*, many are perfectly coherent alternatives to views now in vogue.

The second view is agnosticism, according to which we simply do not know whether consciousness is natural, because of the significant gap between the objective point of view we get in science and the subjective point of view in which consciousness consists. It is not that consciousness is forever beyond our theoretical ken, but rather that we do not know whether we can rope it in, or, for that matter, how we might try.

Third is mysterianism, according to which consciousness, though natural, cannot be understood by us in naturalist terms. It is a mystery. Certain properties of the brain account for it, but whatever we discover about them, and however hard we try to understand consciousness in terms of them, we will never be able to do so. Creatures of more sophisticated intelligence might be able to solve the problem, but we cannot. The solution is cognitively closed to us, because we can only seek it in one of two mutually exclusive and severally inadequate ways, scientifically or philosophically. Lab work leaves no room for consciousness as such, and armchair work renders lab notes irrelevant, which, surely, they are not. In this book, I leave each of these views—anti-naturalism, agnosticism, and mysterianism—as live but bracketed options. I will not have much to say about them, except indirectly. Suffice it to say, they are rather too pessimistic about the prospects for a theory of consciousness.

Before getting down to the business of developing such a theory of consciousness, it might be helpful to have a better sense of what that business is. I begin by discussing blindsight and various things psychologists have said about it, including certain scientific hypotheses which are of keen, if often ignored, philosophical interest. Then I examine a host of cases similar to blindsight to determine how blindsight should be described; this bears significantly on the question of how to explain such phenomena and, more importantly, what conclusions we may draw from them. Following this, I address various controversial arguments to the effect that, despite how things seem, consciousness does not really exist. Some of these arguments turn on blindsight, which, it turns out, makes a much stronger case for conscious realism. Next, I criticize the view that, again, despite how things seem, consciousness *cannot* be involved in producing thought or action, after which I explore the idea that consciousness, after all, is so involved, taking this seemingly trivial truth, step by step, to a very unpopular view, one long thought doomed in the philosophy of mind, and which I hope to resuscitate here: a thoroughgoing materialism that anchors mental properties to the world no less securely than physical properties. Rounding off my discussion of consciousness are speculations about how to approach the dreaded hard problem, that of making a naturalist approach to consciousness not so much plausible as intelligible. Finally, I consider applications of blindsight to theories of knowledge and perception respectively. Just as blindsight pops up at the crossroads of scientific and philosophical investigations of consciousness, so too, I argue, does it bear fruit in these other areas of joint concern.

A BRIEF HISTORY OF BLINDSIGHT

I n   t h e   m i d - 1 9 7 0 s , several papers with sober titles were published in equally sober journals like *Nature* and *Brain*.[1] They announced the discovery of a new phenomenon in vision science. The data, preliminary but telling, concerned people who had suffered brain damage and, because of this, had lost the capacity for conscious vision. Despite this handicap, they seemed to retain a significant degree of visual function, leading Lawrence Weiskrantz, perhaps the phenomenon's foremost investigator, to dub it *blindsight*. The name stuck, and, although the early studies on this aptly named condition were later confirmed and considerably augmented, they generated much controversy indeed. How could these people "see" without *seeing?* Avenues of neuroscientific explanation were and are available. But the very idea disturbs the mind. It rings incoherent. Some researchers have raised doubt about whether the phenomenon even exists. Others have speculated about the possibility of blindsight in normal perceivers, who have, at the very least, analogues of it. Still others have explored how blindsight bears on questions of animal consciousness and the neural correlates of human consciousness. Such debates in psychology, some of them with evident philosophical appeal, are the subject of this chapter, as are the many fascinating features of the phenomenon itself. To begin, I will say a little more about certain details of the condition and what it is like to have it than most philosophers do. My thumbnail sketch is designed to give not only an idea of what the phenomenon is, but a flavour of the research tradition that led to its discovery.

We begin almost a century ago with the first studies of vision in people with damaged primary visual cortex, which is at the back of the brain, the occipital lobe, also known as V1, striate cortex, and area 17.[2] Such damage can be caused by things like trauma, vascular accident, disease, tumor, surgical excision, and so on. The term "cortically blind" was coined to describe the loss of visual consciousness resulting from such damage. For a long time it was supposed—quite intuitively—that visual function piggybacks on visual experience and that, consequently, one's degree of cortical blindness determines a corresponding degree of visual dysfunction. This is still the way most of us think about vision. No wonder much of the early work on cortical blindness focused on residual conscious vision. What would be the point of looking for anything else? The first significant results predate the baptism of blindsight by some 40 years. In the 1930s, cortically blind monkeys were found to exhibit pupillary and blinking reflexes thought limited to normal vision. This is hardly a shock on reflection, but in the 1940s it was discovered that such monkeys had residual vision well beyond reflexive responses to unseen stimuli. They could detect the presence of stimuli, locate them, and discriminate their shape, pattern, orientation, motion, and even colour—all sight unseen.[3] This last ability is perhaps the most surprising, for one would think that colour perception, of all things, just could not be done in the absence of visual experience.

The early test results on decorticated monkeys were replicated and complemented perhaps most importantly by the work of Nicholas Humphrey.[4] He worked for many years with Helen, arguably the star monkey of vision research. Although cortically blind, she was able to navigate her environment and pick up objects with a skill comparable to that of her normally sighted counterparts. But how do we know that monkeys like Helen are cortically blind? How do we know that they lack visual experience? After all, they cannot tell us so. The short answer is that, in addition to behaving in ways that indicate visual function, they also behave in ways that indicate cortical blindness. They can, in other words, be tested for it. In discrimination tasks, for instance, monkeys can be trained to indicate, by pressing one or another response key, whether or not they see a stimulus presented to their visual field. They can also be taught, in cases where they do not see the stimulus, to "guess" at various of its properties, which they do with such reliability that the scare-quotes are unavoidable. The unfortunate fact is that, for the sake of research, these monkeys had their visual cortices surgically removed. We know the monkeys were cortically blind because we made them that way. At the time, moral compunctions about performing such procedures were not nearly as common, or as intensely felt, as they are today.

Blindsight stands out in sharp relief in humans, who, unlike monkeys, can tell us directly whether or not they see something. Indeed, blindsight was baptized only after its discovery in humans. Like decorticated monkeys, human patients can detect and locate targets and discriminate shape, pattern, orientation, motion, and colour.[5] They can also pick up and even catch objects with a skill comparable to normal perceivers—all without visual consciousness. When left to their own devices, patients behave as if blind, but when forced to choose between a pair of provided options (e.g., "red/green") or cued to the appropriate action (e.g., "Catch!"), they perform with astonishing reliability, up to 100 per cent in some cases. They claim to lack visual experience and, taking themselves to be guessing, are surprised at how well they do. They lack confidence in their judgments altogether, in some cases even when they know how well they do—that is, even when they have good inductive grounds for such confidence. As one might expect, though, patients cannot perform more sophisticated sorts of processing. While they can perceive relationships between a stimulus in the blind field and one in the intact field, they cannot perceive such relationships when both stimuli are unseen. Without some such visual dysfunction, we might hesitate to take patients at their word when they claim to lack visual experience. Not only do we have such evidence, however, but it is also possible to map patients' blind fields precisely. Usually one standardizes a grid of the patient's entire visual field, then moves a light around to various locations corresponding to points on the grid. At each point the patient is asked if the light is visible. If it is, that point on the grid is marked as falling within the intact field; if not, it is marked as falling within the blind field. By successive approximations, the borders of the blind field can be sharply traced.

At this point you might be wondering what it is like to have blindsight. Imagine you wake up in hospital. You see a doctor at the foot of your bed, eyeing you with concern. The lights are too bright, and you are still a bit groggy from the anaesthetic, besides which, your head hurts. So you close your eyes, asking the doctor what happened. She says you have had an accident and had to have brain surgery. Unfortunately, part of your visual cortex was destroyed, but the damage was limited; it could have been much worse. She expects that only part of your visual field has been compromised and that everything else should be normal. Fully awake, your eyes now accustomed to the light, you are relieved to see the shapes and shades of familiar hospital paraphernalia, the industrial paint of the walls, the venetian blinds, the steady drip of an IV. You smile at the doctor, but this does not seem to ease her concern. If anything, she looks at you more intently. She asks if, while looking straight at her and without moving your head, you can see the door, which is to your left. You cannot. Informed of this, the doctor consoles you on being cortically blind in the left half of your visual field. The damage, she says, was to the back right part of your brain. Then you notice it, an asymmetry. Still looking at the doctor, you can see much more to the right of her than you can to the left. Although the rest of your visual field seems normal, it seems to have collapsed on one side. It is not as though there is a swatch of black or grey, like a partial eyepatch, blocking objects from view. It is rather as though the periphery of your visual field has crept inward from the left. You remember having seen things there before the accident, but now there is nothing. Closing one eye, then the other, you notice subtle differences, but what stays the same is that objects just left of centre fade quickly out of consciousness.

Suddenly a thought occurs to you. The doctor did not say you were partially blind, she said you were *cortically* blind. After all, you cannot see a thing in the gap. Move your eyes, and you move the gap, bringing what was obscured into view. But in what way are you not simply blind? Cortical blindness, she tells you, means a lack of visual experience. It does not necessarily mean a lack of visual function, unlike ordinary blindness. Despite the gap in your visual field, you may have, unbeknownst to you, a lot of information about its contents, information not accessible to you but deployable by you in special circumstances. This leaves you even more puzzled than before. How can you have such information without visual experience? More puzzling is how, under any circumstances, you could *use* such information. You decide that the doctor must be trying to trick you, perhaps in some compassionate attempt to distract you from dwelling too much on the injury. But she insists she is not trying to distract you. There are several well-documented cases she has read about. What is more, she says, if you are willing to indulge her, she will run some informal experiments to see if you have this residual vision. Partly incredulous, partly intrigued, and partly just to humour her, you grant the doctor's request.

First the doctor presents a series of flashcards to your blind field, asking you to guess, for each card, whether the stimulus is X- or O-shaped. Seeing nothing and insisting as much to the doctor, you feel disinclined to guess. She asks you to take a stab at it, to go with your gut inclination, however silly it may seem. You do. Another series is presented. This time you are asked to guess whether there is a stimulus on the card. Again you go with your gut, guessing that sometimes there is a stimulus present, other times that there is none. In the next series the doctor asks whether the stimulus is moving to the right or to the left. Nothing you see tips you off, and so again you guess. In the last series you are asked to guess whether the stimulus is red or green. Tabulating the results, the doctor asks you how often you think you were right. About half the time, you bet. After all, you might as well have flipped a coin to decide what to guess. A coin flip would have a 50/50 chance of giving you the right answer, so surely taking a verbal stab would give you the same odds. You must have scored at chance, you think. As if she knows your thoughts, the doctor smiles. It turns out your score was nearly perfect. What seemed like guesswork was anything but. Now although you are sure the doctor is not trying to dupe you, that she seems sincere and appears to know what she is doing, you remain somewhat skeptical.

In the next experiment the doctor puts different objects on a table in your blind field, asking you to reach for each in turn. The objects differ in shape, size, orientation, and location on the table—a coffee cup on the right, a ruler held vertical in the back left corner, a baseball in the centre. Just as you took a verbal stab in the flashcard series, here you take a manual stab. And yet your hand seems to know where it is supposed to go, adjusting to the shape, size, orientation, and position of each object. Putting a wrinkle in the experiment, the doctor tosses a nerf ball at you, making sure it stays in the blind field throughout its trajectory. You do not move a muscle, and it bounces off you harmlessly. Again the nerf ball is thrown, but this time the doctor says "Catch!" and not only do you move to catch it, you do in fact catch it. Here there is no question of being duped, barring a fantastic kind of skepticism. What you thought would be fumbling is too precise to be fumbling. Your shots in the dark betray excellent marksmanship. When left to your own devices, the blind field is useless. Under the right conditions, however, you perform with astonishing reliability and skill. You have blindsight.

Now that you have some idea of what it is like to have blindsight, a few further remarks about the blind field are in order. So far I have been speaking as if there are large, uniform gaps in the visual field. They are large, typically, and they are gaps, but they often include small irregularities. Because patients' brain damage is accidental, or the byproduct of medical intervention, in many cases the V1 corresponding to the blind field is not completely destroyed. One of the first and most extensively studied patients, known in the literature as DB, has a small island of fuzzy conscious vision in his blind field, while another, GY, has a peninsula of normal vision jutting out from his intact field. Even setting aside such irregularities, blind fields are not, strictly speaking, always blind. Patients sometimes report a minimal awareness of what is going on in the blind field proper, especially with fast-moving or high-contrast stimuli. GY, for instance, sometimes has a vague awareness that "something's going on," other times he "just knows" what is going on. In these cases, he either lacks sensory experience altogether or is unable to describe such experience as he has. In other cases, he has proto-visual experiences, say, of the motion of a stimulus, which he is able to describe quite well.[6] While for the most part such minimal awareness does not impede patients' performance—sometimes it does—it is important to note that blindsight *per se*, or classic blindsight if you will, occurs only when no such awareness is reported and is, moreover, denied. Otherwise it is what you might call "purblindsight."

While it is clear that damage to V1 is what causes cortical blindness in blindsight patients, what is not so clear is how, neurologically speaking, patients do what they do. There is nothing metaphysically peculiar here: it is the brain that does the work. But how does the information get through? This is a matter of some debate.[7] In normal perceivers, most information received by the retina passes through V1 on its way to other cortical areas. But in blindsight this route seems cut off, so it is only natural to think that some other neural pathway must be involved. As it turns out, there *is* another fairly significant pathway, one that bypasses V1 on its way to other parts of the brain. One hypothesis is that this other route, the tectopulvinar pathway, underwrites blindsight. Another is that, on the contrary, the V1 route is not completely compromised: spared islands of V1 cortex let the information through. Right away, the first hypothesis might sound more plausible, for surely these spared islands of cortex account for the blind field irregularities mentioned above—DB's island of fuzzy conscious vision, GY's normal peninsula. Not exactly. Spared V1 does account for both irregularities, yet the correspondence is less than perfect. One patient, CLT, was found to exhibit blindsight in an area corresponding to an active island of spared V1 cortex. This does not mean, however, that the second hypothesis is true. V1 neurons are highly specialized, and it is unlikely that the few islands of spared V1 could be responsible for blindsight in areas whose corresponding V1 is gone. GY was found to exhibit blindsight without activation of any spared V1, as did monkeys whose V1 was entirely removed. We may be wary of drawing conclusions about the human visual system from experiments on monkeys, but vision science proceeds best in reflective equilibrium between both kinds of primate.

Perhaps the most heated debate about blindsight among psychologists concerns whether the phenomenon exists at all.[8] Some critics think, mistakenly, that in order for blindsight to be a genuine phenomenon, it *must not* involve V1. But this is a separate issue. Whether blindsight involves V1 is a matter of explaining the phenomenon, and, whichever explanation fits, the phenomenon wins. Another criticism is that blindsight is underwritten by spared islands of V1, but, as we have just seen, the current evidence weighs against this possibility. Yet another suggestion is that, owing to the eye's optical properties, light from the blind field may scatter to intact field receptors, being processed from there covertly. However, this can be controlled for by making sure that, even with maximal scatter, the light still falls on blind field receptors. Another worry is that blindsight is merely a degraded form of normal vision, an artifact of patients using different response criteria. They may be aware of stimulus properties without counting such awareness as seeing. As already mentioned, however, such "purblindsight" is experimentally distinguishable from blind-sight proper. And if blindsight proper involved degraded conscious-ness, we would expect that the less degraded the consciousness, the better the performance. Instead, patients sometimes perform *worse* with proto-experiences than without. Owing to the limited number and availability of blindsight patients and to a few failed attempts to test them, other worries concern whether blindsight experiments are replicable, replicability being the noble benchmark of good science. These concerns have been largely assuaged, however, by replicating the experiments. Much of the skepticism about blindsight, I suggest, is based on theoretically motivated or commonsense misgivings about the conceptual integrity of the very idea. But "sight" without *sight* wel-comes no such misgivings. I have admittedly run roughshod over these concerns, but although it is important to be aware of them, and of how they have been answered, it is wise not to tarry too long in matters that are, or ought to be, all but settled, especially with so much inter-esting stuff to come. Blindsight is a bona fide phenomenon. For those who cannot leave it at that and want to study these debates in earnest, the footnote above will guide you.

Other questions about blindsight concern definition and scope.[9] In fact, one source of resistance to the phenomenon has been its alleged undefinability. This is a curious reason for dismissal. There is no defi-nition of art that satisfies everyone, not as yet anyway; maybe it cannot be defined. But that is no reason to deny that artworks—novels and paintings and sculpture and such—exist. Besides, there are perfectly good, standard definitions in the literature. Blindsight can be defined, for our purposes, as *residual vision in a blind field without concomitant aware-ness*. This definition rules out so-called blindsight in normal perceivers.

You can rig up visual displays in which people reliably discriminate unseen stimuli, essentially a form of subliminal perception. The difference is that with subliminal perception, there is normal visual experience behind which covert information sneaks in. Peripheral vision is a similarly analogous case, although here we expect little or no consciousness, whereas blindsight is pretty clearly vision without *expected* visual consciousness. Whether the term "blindsight" ought to be applied to include such cases is a terminological quibble. The urge to more elastic usage is understandable and even, in a certain sense, appropriate, but when I speak of blindsight in this book, I mean it in the narrow, more technical sense. Dispensing with the quibble, then, we can turn to questions of a more palpable significance.

What, for instance, does blindsight suggest about animal consciousness? Surprisingly, there has been little speculation about this among philosophers. One surprising claim is that blindsight undermines the notion of animal consciousness.[10] Since blindsight patients discriminate stimulus properties unawares, it is thought that they must have some kind of perceptual experience without knowing that they do; otherwise, they would not be so reliable in "guessing" at stimulus properties. Thus, an analogy between blindsight and animal perception can be drawn: simply put, animal perception is like blindsight. Ignoring the conceptual difficulties inherent in talk of unconscious consciousness, the upshot is that animals do not have, and cannot have, the kind of raw perceptual consciousness that humans do. Animals, strictly speaking, are not conscious at all. The use of blindsight here is particularly ironic, since it relies on distinguishing blindsight and animal vision as a kind of blindsight from normal human vision. If this is right, blindsight, as a kind of aberrant vision, must be a uniquely *human* phenomenon. However, it is not. As we have seen, much of what we know about blindsight comes from studying monkeys who have been surgically tailored for the phenomenon; therefore, it is not a uniquely human condition. I have always marvelled at how the human species, in an effort to distinguish itself, would deny other species outright what they so clearly possess in some measure—tool use, reasoning ability, language understanding, moral significance, and, yes, even perceptual consciousness.

Blindsight also tells us something about the neural correlates of consciousness, at least of visual consciousness. If blindsight involves, as it seems to, no V1, this suggests that V1 is crucial for visual consciousness. It *is* the primary visual cortex, after all. This does not mean that V1 is *sufficient* for visual consciousness, but it does indicate that V1 is *necessary* for visual consciousness. It is insufficient because, in terms of perceptual anatomy, it is too basic a structure. Also, as already discussed, there is evidence of blindsight with respect to active islands of spared V1. Consciousness comes further up the line, possibly in area 46, a prefrontal nexus of many pathways, a visual crossroads, as it were. V1 is not, of course, necessary for the vague awareness and proto-visual consciousness of patients presented with fast-moving or high-contrast stimuli. But the vague awareness reported by patients is more cognitive than sensory, a knowing *that* without an experience *of.* Proto-visual consciousness is, however, clearly sensory. Indeed, there is evidence that visual consciousness without V1 is possible, and if area 46 is sufficient and can be stimulated without V1-mediation—a sort of visual-brain-in-a-vat scenario—then, in principle and in practice, it must be possible. The moral is that visual consciousness is V1-dependent, give or take "purblindsight" and the artificial stimulation of area 46. In other words, *normal* visual consciousness is V1-dependent in naturally functioning human brains.

This may not seem all that significant. Did we not know that already, and do we not, ideally, want to discover the neural correlates of consciousness *tout court*, not just those in some particular sense modality? Maybe so, but what we have learned from blindsight can usefully complement hypotheses about the neural correlates of consciousness *tout court*. There are several of these.[11] One proposal, owing to Crick and Koch, is that consciousness consists in neural oscillations in the 40-hz range, in which case visual consciousness might be generated by 40-hz oscillations in area 46. Another proposal, offered by Bernard Baars, is that consciousness is a sort of "global workspace" where information is widely available to other parts of the brain. If so, visual consciousness might be realized by area 46 acting as such a distribution source. Maybe it is the 40-hz oscillations that do the trick; maybe it is something else. But it is *something*. It might seem that blindsight is only of marginal importance to eagerly awaited discoveries about the mind, and that it is all but silent on the hard questions of consciousness. However, if we can speak of blindsight as vision *sans* visual consciousness, then the philosophical pay-off turns out to be rich—much richer, in fact, than many so far have dared allow themselves to speculate.

D ISSOCIATION CASES, like blindsight, are important for improving our understanding of how the brain works. If brain damage leads to a dissociation of function in some domain from the experience normally associated with it, this suggests that the part of the brain that is damaged is necessary for the kind of consciousness which is conspicuously absent, and, if the function is impaired, as in blindsight, this suggests something of the role that consciousness may play in normal function. Not merely of scientific interest, such findings bear on what we say about the mind from a philosophical point of view. Not every armchair agenda will fit the data, once sufficient care is taken in describing the phenomena. Such care is necessary because we want, on the one hand, to avoid hasty, perhaps implausible, explanations of the phenomena at issue. On the other hand, we want the phenomena to be well poised for philosophical application. Inadequate description will not do. In the case of blindsight, the rewards are rich indeed, provided we interpret the phenomenon correctly. In this chapter, I will situate blindsight among a host of dissociation cases to help resolve a particularly striking interpretive dispute in the blindsight literature, thus leaving the phenomenon poised for philosophical application. It will also give you a sense of how dissociation cases generally are both intriguing in themselves and important for understanding how the mind and brain work. In the last chapter blindsight was characterized as residual vision in a blind field without concomitant awareness. The phrase "without concomitant awareness" was meant to rule out cases of what I called "purblindsight," where patients "just know," or have proto-sensations, of what is going on in the blind field. So characterized, blindsight is a bit of a surprise. Our unschooled intuitions tell us that visual function depends, in some sense, on visual experience. Not surprisingly, some psychologists and philosophers have denied that blindsight is as I have described it.[1] They insist that visual function really does depend on visual experience, as common sense tells us. Since blindsight patients disavow experience, they must have, it seems, another kind of experience, one of which they are apparently unaware. "Seeing" without *seeing*, in other words, is not a subtle equivocation, it is an ill-disguised contradiction. The scare-quotes and italics do not help. No doubt blindsight involves sensory and cognitive representations; information does get through. Consciousness is also involved. Patients are aware of what they are supposed to do in experimental trials, of what option they choose when asked, and of what bodily movements they initiate when cued, not to mention their awareness of the questions and cues themselves. But that is not concomitant awareness of blind field information as such. The question is whether the information patients possess and exploit unawares constitutes an odd kind of perceptual experience. Does blindsight involve a peculiar kind of consciousness? Does it *have* to?

This might seem a terminological quibble, and perhaps it is, but it touches on matters of some importance to philosophers and psychologists. Common sense says that the function of visual systems depends on visual consciousness. You can dress up this observation and give it a moniker like "Signal Detection Theory," but the situation remains the same. It is clear that much visual function does not involve consciousness, but rather precedes it. My perception of the coffee cup at my elbow is built up out of simpler components by my visual system. It picks up edges and surfaces more or less directly, but the shape of the cup, as I see it, is an elaborate, though perfectly ordinary piece of neurological architecture. Of course these processes *culminate* in consciousness. I do, after all, see the cup. Even subliminal perception requires liminal cover for covert stimuli, and so vision may yet seem dependent on visual consciousness. But this is precisely the kind of intuition which the discovery of blindsight undermined. As Pat Churchland says, blindsight "knocked the stuffing out of the 'obvious' assumption that awareness of a signal is necessary for an intentional response to that signal."[2] Common sense may help frame the terms, but it is no dictator. What, then, is wrong with the idea that blindsight involves a peculiar kind of consciousness? It is this:

the idea is motivated by common sense and is unabashedly conservative. While conservativeness is, all else being equal, a theoretical virtue, the notion of unconscious consciousness is, to say the least, a conceptual infelicity, one far more *radical* than abandoning the "obvious" assumption that vision depends on consciousness. In the name of common sense, it is better to be a healthy conservative than an unwitting radical.

A particularly nice distinction has been proposed by Owen Flanagan[3] for interpreting dissociation cases and for distinguishing different aspects of normal perceptual and cognitive function. It is a useful distinction, but by no means unique. Though it goes by different names in different regions of the literature, and although many specialists have the luxury of ignoring it, the human sciences are shot through with it, or at least with isomorphs of it. Here it is. We want to distinguish two kinds of sensitivity a system, organic or otherwise, may exhibit, the more basic of which is *informational* sensitivity. To be sensitive in this way means being able to acquire and respond to information about the world. You do not need consciousness to be informationally sensitive. You do not need to be a person or a living being. Motion detectors, barcode scanners, automated banking machines, and the like are informationally sensitive in a minimal sense, although their sensitivity is limited to very specific kinds of information acquired in very specific kinds of ways. Humans, too, have such sensitivity. We are motion detectors, among other things. Much of what the brain does is done on a purely information sensitive basis. But as a species, we are not just informationally sensitive, we are also *experientially* sensitive. To be sensitive in this way is to be conscious. I am informationally sensitive to motion when my visual system detects it, irrespective of what awareness may result. It is when such awareness results that I am experientially sensitive. There is an asymmetric relationship between the two sensitivities. One cannot be experientially sensitive to something without being informationally sensitive to it. The reverse does not necessarily hold, however. Indeed, it seems we experience only a subset of what we are informationally sensitive to. Experience depends on information, not vice versa.

The application of this distinction to blindsight is straightforward. With respect to blind field stimuli, patients are clearly information-ally sensitive. Remember, their shots in the dark betray excellent marksmanship. Their visual systems take in and deploy much information about unseen stimuli. Patients are not, however, experientially sensitive to the stimuli they discriminate. The stimuli are unseen. In "purblindsight," where there is some vague awareness of stimulus properties, patients have a modicum of experiential sensitivity. It is nowhere near that enjoyed by normal perceivers, but it is on the scale. Suspicion may linger that blindsight is underwritten by some form of experience that patients do not notice or, for whatever reason, cannot acknowledge. Consider a case of "hysterical" blindness where, owing to some bizarre, vision-specific neurosis, a patient has experiential sensitivity, but cannot acknowledge it, even to him- or herself. Blindsight, however, is not "merely psychological." There is real brain damage involved, and the damage is clearly sensory, not cognitive. There are cases of experiential sensitivity with compromised cognition, which might be confused with a lack of experiential sensitivity, but these, as we shall see, are distinguishable from blindsight, conceptually as well as empirically. To make this clear and to show the appropriateness of the informational/experiential sensitivity distinction and its application to blindsight, it is time to situate blindsight, as promised, among a host of other dissociation cases.

The first cases are analogues of blindsight in other sensory modes, although these have been studied far less extensively than blindsight.[4] Touch shows a similar dissociability of function from consciousness. Damage to the parietal cortex, at the upper back part of the brain, causes tactile anaesthesia in the corresponding part of the tactual field, just as damage to V1 causes cortical blindness in the corresponding part of the visual field. If the damage is on the left, it is part of the right tactual field that is numb, just as, in blindsight, the blind field and V1 injury are on opposite sides. Despite being cortically numb to tactual stimuli, even quite intense stimuli, patients are nonetheless able to reliably point to where they were touched. Blindfolds and other measures are used to ensure the information is not gathered by other means, such as by a surreptitious peek. The condition has been called "blind touch," but I think "numb touch" would be better. There is nothing remarkable about feeling in the dark. Another sort of numb sense is so-called deaf hearing, where supratemporal damage leaves patients unable to comprehend speech but able, nonetheless, to recognize spoken words in forced-choice tasks similar to those used in blindsight trials. Smell and taste have not yet been tested, perhaps because, as sensory modes, they are too basic to exhibit dissociation, perhaps because the right patients have not shown up. What is going on in blind touch and deaf hearing is this: patients are informationally sensitive to stimuli but experientially insensitive. They "touch" without *touching*, they "hear" without *hearing*. As with blindsight, there is nothing metaphysically funny here. The brain still does the work, but the conscious channels are cut off.

There are also quite selective visual dissociations worth mentioning. They are quite selective in that, while visual function is more or less normal, there is a particular kind of stimulus property patients cannot see.[5] One condition is *achromatopsia*, the inability to see colour, which is caused by brain damage just forward of V1. Achromatopsics see things in various shades of grey, not metaphorically, as some of us are wont to affect from time to time, but literally. (To those of a certain aesthetic bent, myself included, the idea is not completely unappealing.) Achromatopsic patients, despite the loss of conscious colour vision, can, it seems, discriminate colour. They can, for instance, detect edges, or discriminate shapes, where the only means of doing so, given the experimental set-up, is by implicit colour processing. Another selective dissociation concerns the inability of a particular patient, LM, to see motion. The world presents itself to her, not like a black-and-white movie—her colour perception is normal—but as a series of discrete still frames from a technicolour movie, a sort of perpetual slideshow. She has developed various strategies to deal with this disorder. Speed, for instance, can be inferred from relative change in successive stills. Bodily movements can be initiated or modified on the basis of such anticipations as each time slice instills. These strategies cannot work, though, for quick response-time tasks like catching a ball. Even so, LM can catch balls with a skill comparable to that of normal perceivers, just as blindsight patients can. She does not see motion, but she "sees" it, just as achromatopsics "see" colour without seeing it. Both are cases of informational sensitivity without experiential sensitivity. The system gets it, but the subject does not.

Another, somewhat less clear dissociation is neglect, of which there are various kinds. Unilateral neglect typically involves right parietal damage, with corresponding dysfunction in the left visual field. When given a picture and asked to reproduce it, patients only draw the right side. When shown a drawing of two houses, one above the other, as long as the right sides of the drawing are the same, patients will claim that the houses are identical, however markedly they differ on the left side. If, for example, one of the houses is depicted on the left side as burning, with flame and smoke shooting out the window, patients neglect the difference. But if asked which house they would rather live in, silly as the question seems to them, they will "arbitrarily" pick the house that is not on fire.[6] Clearly, such patients have informational sensitivity. What is not so clear is the appropriate verdict on experiential sensitivity. It is not so much that patients are experientially insensitive, but that their experiential sensitivity does not matter. Unlike blindsight patients, they do not notice their own deficient notice. Where the former "see" without *seeing*, the latter seem to see without *noticing*. The seeing does not matter to them. On the other hand, maybe patients do not see at all and simply fail to notice that they do not, as in Anton's syndrome, also known as blindness denial, in which patients deny being visually impaired despite quite obvious failures to see. It is a juicy indeterminacy, especially for those who would undermine anything like a commonsense theory of consciousness. However, we must not ignore two salient facts. One, blindsight is *not* neglect. They are distinguishable conditions, not only neuroscientifically, but also from the patient's point of view. Two, because of this, whatever indeterminacy attaches to neglect, it does not stick to blindsight.

Neglect is, in a certain sense, a form of *agnosia*—patients lack explicit knowledge of the stimulus properties they discriminate. Visual agnosia also comes in more selective forms. Some agnosia patients cannot judge the shape of objects or the orientation of a simple line. They cannot tell if a line is vertical, horizontal, or sloping.

But if a mailbox aperture is rotated to various different angles, patients are pretty good at putting cards in the slot.[7] The patient's hand rotates, almost of its own accord, to the correct orientation. The same is true of shape. If you ask a patient to reach for an object, the reaching hand will, before contact is made, adjust to the object's shape, even though the patient cannot tell what shape it is. Reach for something right now and notice what your hand does in its excursion towards the object. Agnosia patients do the same thing, more or less, only without the knowledge you and I have when we do it. Here again, informational sensitivity is on the job, but here again, too, it might seem that we are faced with an indeterminacy. The lack of knowledge suggests a lack of experiential sensitivity, but, perhaps, as with neglect, there is only a useless sort of experiential sensitivity. The failure, in this event, would be one of cognitive integration. What is experienced and processed covertly on an information sensitive basis cannot lead to normal knowledge extraction. The extractor is broken. As with neglect, however, whatever the correct story happens to be concerning the relationship between experience and sensitivity, the condition is clearly distinguishable from blindsight. If it is ultimately there at all, the indeterminacy is non-transferable.

So far I have discussed cases of perceptual dissociation, but brain damage can cause other dissociations instructive to consider.[8] Some of these involve memory or, rather, the apparent lack thereof. One peculiar condition, *prosopagnosia*, has to do with recognizing faces. Prosopagnosics cannot reliably distinguish faces of people they know, even close friends and family members, from those of complete strangers. They know a face when they see one, and they can tell one face from another, discriminating features and all the rest. The problem is not perceptual, it is mnemonic. They score badly when given a series of faces and asked to tell which ones are familiar and which are not. Nonetheless, the system betrays covert memory: familiar things, especially when they have emotional significance, bring about detectable, measurable changes in certain properties of the skin—galvanic skin responses. When shown a series of faces, a patient exhibits galvanic skin responses at the familiar ones, as we would, but not at the unfamiliar ones. The system remembers what the subject does not.

Another condition has to do with skills learning. One patient, HM, was given the Tower of Hanoi puzzle, which involves moving rings one at a time from one post to another, the object being to stack the rings in a particular order on the last post. HM's learning curve was normal. At first he was frustrated, but then he caught on, and was eventually able to solve the puzzle with ease. The surprising thing is that, owing to his brain damage, HM could not consciously remember new events. His short-term memory was short indeed. Each time he was given the Tower of Hanoi puzzle, it was new to him. He could not recall having tried it before. Nor did he know how to do it. At least, he did not *think* he knew. The system learned and deployed the learning with HM none the wiser. In league with prosopagnosics, he was informationally, but not experientially, sensitive to his memory.

Before blindsight became a hot topic, philosophers were fascinated, and some still are, with another kind of dissociation case, namely that of split-brain patients.[9] HM, in fact, was a split-brain patient. He had suffered from a quite severe form of epilepsy. His seizures would start locally and then spread to full-blown *grand mal*. A procedure often performed in such cases is to sever the *corpus callosum*, the cortical tissue that connects and allows communication between the two cerebral hemispheres. The subcortical structures are left intact. The therapeutic rationale is to contain seizures that otherwise would spread throughout the brain. A *demi-grand* is far less devastating than a *grand*. With interhemispheric communication essentially cut off, very interesting dissociations arise between the left, typically verbal hemisphere, and the right, typically mute. In everyday life, patients behave for the most part normally, although conflict is occasionally exhibited between the unintegratable responses of the two hemispheres. Such conflicts can be made explicit in experimental settings, when patients fixate on a point while different words or images are flashed to the left and right visual fields. Patients verbally report right-field information, which is processed in the left, speech-ready hemisphere, but they deny the presence of stimuli in the left field. Even so, the right brain shows informational sensitivity to left-field stimuli in, for instance, left arm behaviour, which the right brain controls. If shown a key, or the word "key," in the left field, the mute right brain can direct the left hand to draw a key or to pick out a key from a random collection of objects, despite the patient's verbal disavowal of any presented stimuli. Is there experiential sensitivity in the right brain? Is there consciousness? Not obviously, but not obviously *not* either. It is not obviously conscious because, as we know, informational sensitivity does not require as much. It is not obviously not conscious because of the lack of verbal expressibility. Philosophers have speculated about divided consciousness and, perhaps, divided selves in split-brain patients. Such speculation would no doubt be rekindled by confirmation of right brain consciousness. Once we discover the neural correlates of normal consciousness, all we would have to do is see whether they turn up in the right hemisphere of split brains. Such findings, indeed, would help us resolve many outstanding indeterminacies in dissociation cases.

It is not only in damaged brains that dissociations occur. Consider sleepwalking, or the truckdriver effect—on road trips, especially long or familiar ones, one goes on automatic pilot, remembering afterward nothing of the trip taken. Sleepwalking seems to involve unconscious informational sensitivity. The truckdriver effect may be similar, but, plausibly enough, I think it is rather like neglect, where the experiential sensitivity simply does not matter enough to be fixed in memory, not because of neuropathology, but because of fatigue, distraction, boredom, etc. Other cases, mentioned earlier, include subliminal perception and peripheral vision. I have said about as much as I want to about the former, and how blindsight differs from it, but a few further remarks about the latter are in order. As one approaches the outer edge of the visual field, it seems that consciousness diminishes faster than certain perceptual capacities, motion perception in particular. Imagine you are walking along and all of a sudden, reflexively, you duck, and you notice, just as you duck, something zipping past your head, a bird or insect, maybe a frisbee. It would, it seems, have hit you if you had not ducked. Such experiences are not uncommon. What can we make of them? It certainly seems that the visual system is responding on a reflexive, information-sensitive basis before awareness catches up—awareness after the fact, if you will. However, I certainly do not want to stake much of a claim on this anecdotal sense of things. Perhaps a minimal sort of consciousness is involved after all. You may make peripheral notice which, because of the urgency to duck, you cannot subsequently recall. There may also be subtle auditory cues that tip you off that something is heading your way.

Normal perceivers exhibit similar, though less ordinary, phenomena in certain experimental settings.[10] One example is metacontrast. If a small circular stimulus, a disc, is flashed briefly in a subject's visual field, she will report seeing it. But if the first stimulus is followed by a second, a ring, the innermost edge of which coincides with the outermost edge of the disc, she will only report seeing the ring. Even though the ring masks the earlier appearance of the disc, the subject can reliably guess whether there were, in fact, two stimuli. The information gets through. The information also gets through in what is called the Broadbent filtering effect: subjects are given a set of earphones and told to listen only to one channel, where they hear an ambiguous sentence, such as, "The lieutenant put out the lantern to signal the attack." On the unattended channel, there is noise, along with a sentence that disambiguates the attended sentence, either "He extinguished the flame" or 'He put the lantern outside." Although the subject reports hearing nothing salient on the noise channel, they show a marked interpretive preference for the unattended meaning of "put out." What is going on? Is the sensitivity purely informational, or is there a flash of conscious sensitivity that does not matter? It might seem that we could never know, that either decision would be arbitrary, and that perhaps there is something misleading about the very formulation of the question. Again, once we know more about the neural correlates of normal consciousness, we will have a much better idea of what to look for in exotic cases like these. Perhaps one, the other, both, or neither will involve a brief flash of conscious sensitivity. The importance of dissociation cases for the study of consciousness is, I think, obvious. With notable exceptions, however, philosophers of mind have only recently begun to take this idea seriously. Each dissociation case discussed above has been marshalled against consciousness, and the distinction between informational and experiential sensitivity is a useful first means of redress, even in cases which, for now, are interpretively open. The nice thing about blindsight is that it is *not* an ambiguous case. There is nothing ambiguous about residual vision without concomitant awareness. Whatever the neural correlates of consciousness are, you will not find them in blindsight. The phenomenon is now poised for philosophical extraction.

3

S OMETIMES WHEN GIVING A LECTURE, I stop talking and do something silly—perform an absurd dance or utter nonsense syllables in a Monty-Pythonish voice. Then I ask my students why I have done such a silly thing. Is it because I am a silly person, or because I want to illustrate a point and believe I can do so by performing such an absurd act? The point is that knowing what someone wants and believes helps make sense of what they do. Citing the right mental states after the fact helps explain behaviour. Citing them in advance helps predict it. My students show up to class expecting me to be there, because they know that I want, among other things, to be paid, and as Woody Allen said, the secret of success is showing up. This explanatory and predictive apparatus is not unusual, but part of our shared, commonsense view of how the world works. Philosophers call it "folk psychology," the psychology of ordinary folk, folk like you and me. Taking others as conscious and ascribing conscious states to them are important parts of this apparatus, which, when it comes to dealing with human beings, seems inevitable. The most vexingly clever use of blindsight targets these commonsense assumptions, the ultimate aim being, believe it or not, to undermine the mind, to eliminate it from our inventory of what the universe contains. This is *eliminativism*—the view that, strictly speaking, there are no minds. Its main proponents are Paul Churchland and Pat Churchland, and, among their many attacks on the mind, I will discuss two here. One, which targets consciousness, is an argument from blindsight. The other is more of a strategy for undermining folk psychology in general, a strategy I like to call the eliminativist gambit. In this chapter, I will defend the folk on both fronts, the mind on both counts.

What my targets have in common, apart from their surname and antimentalist agenda, is a deep respect for and wide acquaintance with research in psychology and the neurosciences. This affords them a palpable advantage, that of the expert. Few philosophers of mind are as well versed in empirical research. The sheer weight of it is overwhelming, and the edge it gives them is twofold. First, because they know more than many of their colleagues about related domains, even their antagonists are inclined to take them at their word in reporting and interpreting research. This also allows them to rely unduly on their expertise. Arguments are at worst replaced and at best obscured by scientific journalism. Armchair work can profit from such research, but it does not follow that philosophy can be replaced by it or that philosophical concerns obscure rather than illuminate empirical work and the foundations for it. What strikes one about the Churchlands is the profound disrespect they seem to have for their own discipline. Philosophy is held in such low esteem that most of its problems—including the mind/body problem—are predicted to be solved, more or less independently, by science. Just how eliminating the mental, or most of its salient features, will solve the mind/body problem remains unclear.

The Churchlands take blindsight to show that consciousness is not, and cannot become, scientifically respectable. Our concept of consciousness has become so "transmuted" by empirical research that nothing of it will remain in the wake of a complete neuroscience. They are quick to observe that blindsight is strikingly counterintuitive. It is a shock to learn that colour perception, of all things, can occur in the absence of visual experience. Together with other dissociation cases, such as those discussed in the last chapter, this suggests to the Churchlands that our commonsense notion of consciousness is far off the mark, so much so that revision of it in light of empirical evidence will transform it beyond recognition. They prophesy that consciousness is doomed to eventual omission from the inventory of extant things. Is it? Without question, blindsight is a shock to the system, as startling perhaps as the indeterminacies of quantum mechanics. But revising our view of what we need consciousness *for* need not alter our view of what consciousness *is*, vague and incomplete though the view may be. These obligations are distinct, and blindsight only imposes the former. Showing this will not scotch the Churchlands' overall project, but it will undermine part of it and cast some aspersion on the rest.

To fully subject the Churchlands to critical scrutiny would seem to require going over the mass of empirical work on which they report and rely. However, difficult to discern as they sometimes are, general arguments emerge from their work, arguments they claim are supported by reports from the lab, but which can nonetheless be criticized independently. As well as undermining their use of blindsight, I will also show why these more general arguments fail. The vision these arguments are meant to serve is truly optimistic. It is downright utopian. Neuroscience—that is, *utopian* neuroscience—is supposed to replace, without residue, all commonsense notions of mind. Consciousness—along with beliefs, desires, and other intentional states—will fall by the wayside of good scientific ontology. So it is hoped. The main argument for this view rests on the idea that commonsense notions of mind—comprised by folk psychology—constitute merely a first effort to understand ourselves, an understanding amounting to nothing more than making sense of our behaviour. Since first efforts at understanding are dismal failures, and since folk psychology is such a first effort, it is very likely false. Against this, I argue that present-day folk psychology is not at all our first pass at making sense of human behaviour. More importantly, mentality is not posited merely to make sense of behaviour; it is no less part of what has to be explained.

Whereas some philosophers construct blindsight-based thought experiments to attack consciousness, the Churchlands are happy to use plain blindsight for the same end. Blindsight, they claim, is a shock to the system. Commonsense notions of mind cannot, in the end, accommodate it, because of the fact that it is a strikingly counterintuitive phenomenon. Though I agree that blindsight is counterintuitive, the extent to which it is should perhaps not be exaggerated. The layperson already admits vision without visual consciousness, at least in the form of subliminal perception. I have found, however, that the notion of vision without *any* visual consciousness does rattle the uninformed, lay or learned. However, the issue is less how counterintuitive blindsight is and more what revisions, if any, it suggests or forces in our conception of consciousness.

Together with other dissociative phenomena, many of which were discussed in the last chapter, blindsight supposedly transmutes our notion of consciousness beyond recognition.[1] We tend to think that visual function really does depend on visual consciousness. Even subliminal perception requires conscious stimuli behind which subliminal stimuli can sneak into the cognitive system. In blindsight there are no experiences to provide explicit, or to hide covert, information. So we are wrong to suppose that vision requires visual consciousness. We must deny consciousness one of the properties commonsense ascribes it, namely, that it is necessary for visual function. The more such evidence accrues, the more conceptual revisions will be necessary. In the ideal limit, under the auspices of a complete neuroscience, these revisions will have so radically changed our notions of consciousness and other kinds of mental states that no residua of them will remain. That, anyway, is the story.

Now, what exactly is the argument here? If there is consciousness, then all, or at least the bulk, of our intuitions about it are correct—nothing revealed by empirical study of the mind should surprise us. But blindsight does surprise us, thus showing our intuitions to be false and consciousness to be unreal. Of course, it is not blindsight alone but blindsight among other dissociation cases that is supposed to show up the realist. The suspect premise, of course, is the conditional. It would be presumptuous to think that all, or even the bulk, of one's intuitions are correct. But even granting that this is true in many cases, it is bizarre to say that the existence of what one has intuitions about depends on those intuitions being correct. In the case of consciousness, it should suffice that some of our intuitions prove defensible. This eliminativist argument, as I have formulated it, cannot help but seem a strawman. Because it does not seem very persuasive, perhaps it is better to consider the question of conceptual revision.

It is quite unclear what revisions blindsight suggests, much less forces, in our notion of consciousness. If we are wrong to think that vision requires visual consciousness or that visual function wholly depends on visual experience, this still does not suggest a radical revision in our notion of what consciousness *is*, vague and incomplete though the notion may be. Rather, it alters our view of what we need consciousness *for*. What needs revising, if anything, is our view of perceptual processes, and such revision is not radical—if it even counts as a revision. All it says is that some behaviorally effective visual function is independent of visual experience. Here is an analogy. Nuclear fusion requires temperatures in the extreme order of what stars and H-bombs generate. It needs a fusion reactor, in other words, natural or otherwise. Suppose that cold fusion had turned out to be a genuine phenomenon. If so, we would have to acknowledge that fusion could occur in the absence of fusion reactors, so conceived. But this would not change our theory of what suns and H-bombs do, nor would it call into question their existence! In the same way, blindsight alters nothing in our conception of consciousness, nor does it call into question its ontological status.

Perhaps I am overstating the case somewhat. Blindsight makes us deny that visual experience has one of the properties formerly ascribed to it, just as cold fusion would make us deny that fusion reactors have one of the properties currently ascribed to them—namely, their being necessary for vision and fusion, respectively. So there is a sense in which the concept of consciousness has changed, and a sense in which the concept of fusion would change. These conceptual changes, however, do not touch the core of either concept. Fusion reactors would still be understood as the things that conjoin atomic nuclei under extreme temperatures, just as consciousness is a matter of the ways things seem to a subject. That neither is necessary for the work it does does nothing to upbraid them.

Suppose that blindsight did force the conceptual revolution the Churchlands anticipate, and we had a neuroscience that explained human behaviour perfectly. In this ideal theory, consciousness is replaced by its appropriate successor—let us call it *schmonsciousness*—defined in purely neurological terms. Either consciousness will be a recognizable ancestor of schmonsciousness, or it will not. If so, then schmonsciousness theory will constitute not an elimination of, but a good theory of, consciousness, a sharpening of our present-day notion not out of, but into, the currency it so richly deserves. If not, we will no longer be practicing psychology, which is, after all, the ardent hope of the eliminativist. But if schmonsciousness really is an appropriate successor, it will be recognizable as such. The lineage will be traceable. If it were insisted that, even so, there is no consciousness, consider that utopian neurology itself would be psychology's legitimate heir *only* if it could explain all that psychology seeks to explain, including consciousness. My claim that psychology seeks to explain more than mere behaviour stands in stark contrast to the key arguments for eliminativism. If my claim is true, none of them works.

Eliminativism attacks the mental on three fronts. The first move is to argue that folk psychology, together with the mental states it postulates in its explanatory apparatus, is a wide, if not systematic, failure. The second is to argue that, since first attempts to account for phenomena are invariably failures, our first attempt to explain human behaviour—folk psychology—is very likely false, and this falsehood points inevitably to dispensing with the intentional states and phenomenal experiences to which its explanations appeal. The third move is to argue that the smooth reduction of mental states to brain states is extremely unlikely and that, consequently, the mental cannot fit into a comprehensive, scientifically respectable worldview. Remember earlier, when I talked about anchoring the mind to the physical world in the way we should ideally want? That is what a smooth reduction would do. Taken together, these moves constitute the eliminativist gambit, a gambit which, I argue, is unsuccessful, as is each move it comprises.

Somewhat surprisingly, the supposed failure of folk psychology is not assigned to the predictive uncertainty of ascribing mental states to other people or to limits on the extent to which behaviour can be made sense of by such ascription. Folk psychology is alleged to fail not because it seems that, however competently we ascribe mental states to people, they can surprise our best expectations. Nor is it alleged to fail because some behaviour, from the eccentric to the insane, is difficult to rationalize. Rather, its failure is seen in the fact that it cannot explain "what sleep is" or "how differences in intelligence are grounded," much less "how memory works" or "what mental illness is"[2] (emphasis removed). What will explain these, along with the phenomena on which folk psychology has *some* explanatory purchase, is a perfected neuroscience.

First of all, it is unclear that *folk* psychology does, or ought to, include any of the above in the scope of what it has to explain. Sleep, for instance, and the roles it plays in the lifecycles of organisms, are clearly biological phenomena, best suited for biological explanation, although dreams, and certain effects of sleep deprivation, are admittedly psychological. It is hard to see how neuroscience, by itself, could explain sleep, though it has aided our understanding of certain aspects of sleep, in particular neurophysiological dream phenomena. The others—intelligence, memory, and mental illness—do fall within the scope of folk psychology, but not exclusively, nor does the burden of accounting for them fall on it. It falls instead on *scientific* psychology, which includes, but is not limited to, the neurosciences, as well as other disciplines. Scientific psychology tries to make many folk concepts scientifically tractable, but it has some leeway in modifying folk predicates and much leeway in making finer-grained distinctions among them, discovering lawful connections between them, and modelling those connections. To say that folk psychology fails for not taking up the scientific slack it was never intended to handle seems to force a false dichotomy: folk psychology *or* neuroscience, but not both.

If the point were pressed that, nonetheless, scientific psychology is somehow folk-infected, so that the present "failures" of psychology are surmountable with the overthrow of these folk-infected concepts, what could we say? For one, we could highlight the enormous burden this puts on even a utopian neuroscience. A perfect neuroscience would have to be a revolution not only in the theory of behaviour but also in theories of meaning, knowledge, and rationality. Beliefs, desires, and, to a lesser degree, experiences are indispensable for rationalizing behaviour. More importantly, the fact that scientific psychology has a long road ahead bodes no more ill than the fact that neuroscience does. Is physics a failure just because it harbours a deep, perhaps unresolvable, incompatibility between quantum mechanics and general relativity? Of course not. Frankly, psychology seems to lack the kind of fundamental schism that makes physics so hard.

The second move, which I take to be the primary argument for eliminativism, is an attempt to draw an inductive moral from the history of science, in which the pseudo-scientific posits of moderately successful folk theories are eventually supplanted by the advent of scientifically adequate theories. The argument goes like this. First attempts to explain anything have invariably been failures, and as folk psychology is a first pass at explaining human behaviour, it is probably false. Caloric, an unobservable fluid substance, was once posited to explain various phenomena associated with heat, such as thermal conduction. Phlogiston, an unobservable gaseous substance, was once posited to explain how wood burns and why metal rusts. Similarly, mental states are posited to explain human behaviour, as when my felt pain explains my saying "Ouch!" although they are unobservable, at least from third-person perspectives. But no one nowadays believes in caloric or phlogiston. With the advent of thermodynamics and theories of combustion and oxidization, science did not need them anymore and so dispensed with them accordingly. So, too, will a perfect neuroscience dispense with consciousness and other mentalia.

One problem with these analogies is that conscious states are indeed observable, albeit in a peculiar way. They are observable from a first-person perspective, at least. If materialism is true, they are also observable as brain states. If consciousness is merely dependent on the brain, then it is a real if somewhat utopian possibility that a subject's conscious states could be replicated in another, by replicating, to the extent neural idiosyncrasies allow, the right brain states. Experiences might well be third-person replicable in phenomenal type if not strictly third-person observable in phenomenal token. But the basic point is that consciousness cannot be likened to caloric and phlogiston. To follow the analogy, it is akin not to phlogiston, but to rust. Conscious states are not mere posits for explaining behaviour, they are also, at the same time—and perhaps more importantly—things to be explained. The importance of this point will soon become evident.

The eliminativist has two strategies for dealing with this. The first is to liken mental states not just to outmoded unobservables but to outmoded observables once thought plain to the eye. For example, at one time, disturbed or especially willful women were deemed to be witches: witchiness "explained" their behaviour. Stargazers saw that stars seemed to move around Polaris, as if fixed on some solid, quintessential sphere. Witches and the quintessential sphere were once thought plain to the eye, and yet both have been eliminated from our inventory of the universe. In a like manner, the mind will also vanish. The problem here is that, although the behaviour of women and the movement of stars were and are observable, neither the property of witchiness nor the quintessential sphere can be seen. Plain to the eye or not, they are not akin to consciousness.

So much for the first strategy. The second strategy is to insist on the controversial idea that *all* observation is theory-laden, including acquaintance with one's own conscious states. This means, in effect, that what you see is shaped largely by what you think. The existence of mental states seems obvious, but only because it is built into our current theory of human behaviour. Since acquaintance with conscious states is mediated by the theory presupposing them, the right neurological successor theory will divest us of the folk prejudices that currently make such divestment seem inconceivable. It is not only what you see but whether you see at all that becomes questionable. This strategy, like the first, is unsuccessful. First, it implies that a necessary condition for sentience is the possession, literally, of a theory that posits phenomenal experience. It may be that having consciousness goes hand in hand with at least minimal cognitive capacities, but is it not absurd to suppose that many animals, which are no doubt sentient, possess a *theory* of mind? This brings up an important point. Conscious states are not so much observable as they are the media of observation. This is not to say that consciousness is necessary for perception. Blindsight shows this to be false. Since consciousness is necessary for observation, even if observation is theory-laden, it is also consciousness-laden, and the theoretical dependency of the first is non-transferable.

If what I have said is correct, then the analogies commonly adduced in support of eliminativism fail. The inductive argument they are meant to support fails for similar reasons. The argument, again, is that since folk psychology is a first attempt to explain behaviour, and since first efforts at explanation have always been superceded, so, too, will folk psychology and any theory that incorporates the explanatory apparatus of mental states be superceded. What I want to focus on is the first premise, because there are at least two things wrong with it. Folk psychology, as it stands today, is hardly a first theory. Mental processing was once thought to be associated with the heart, not the brain. Only recently have most ordinary people entertained, much less accepted, that there are unconscious mental states, the explanatory and predictive value of which depends on their being so. On the more abstruse side, the most important insights into the logical structure of mental states are less than 100 years old. Our current understanding of folk concepts is much richer and more refined than it used to be. Of course the Churchlands will insist that the concepts themselves are at issue, not the richness and refinement in our understanding of them. Refinements in our understanding of consciousness and other psychological states may not touch the core of folk concepts, but they do remove any whiff of preliminary effort from present-day folk psychology.

Debates about consciousness really amount to debates about the domain of psychology. Even if present-day folk psychology were a first theory, it would be a mistake to construe it—or scientific psychology—as designed for the sole purpose of explaining behaviour. The domain of psychology comprises both neural and first-person phenomena, even if the latter are identified with a subset of the former. This is not only because experimental theories of mind are expressed and, ultimately, justified in the mind of the experimenter. A good psychology will furnish an apparatus for explaining not just behavioural but primarily mental phenomena and, therefore, will have to make sense *of* as well as *from* a subject's perspective, adequately informed. It is a good bet that mental states systematically affect behaviour, but we have more reason than that to hold that they exist. They are no less things to be explained than part of the explanation.[3] The right psychoneural profiles will allow experimenters to explain the behaviour and psychology of others, together with their own. Not only will the conceptual apparatus be tractable to the experiment's perspective, its scope will include that very perspective, allowing her to account for her own psychological states, including consciousness.

So far I have responded to the first two moves in the eliminativist gambit. The third move is to claim that the smooth reduction of mental states to brain states is a dim prospect, the consequence being that the mind cannot fit into a scientific worldview. Without straight-forward *type* identifications with brain states—where, for example, pain is realized by one and only one type of brain state—we should discard the mental. But this completely ignores the sustained work of non-reductive materialists, the upshot of which is that mere *token* identifications suffice to secure not only the reality of the mental, but also the relative autonomy of psychology.[4] Pain, on this view, is realized not by a single type of brain state, but by brain states of different kinds, one kind on one occasion, another on another, the types corresponding one-to-many rather than one-to-one. If this is enough to secure the physical reality of the mental, then even if the Churchlands are right about the relationship between mental and physical types, this does not force the realist to give up the ghost.[5]

My present concern is not to motivate these versions of materialism, since the eliminativist ignores them in making this move. I suggest, rather, that the reduction might not be so rough after all. One idea, to be explored later, is that mental and neural types are not specified independently but, at least partly, on a mutually informative basis. We typify brain states and processes, in part, on the basis of how well candidate types correspond to mental types.[6] Part of the reason we think of V1 as the primary visual cortex is that stimulating it causes visual experience, while damaging it takes away visual experience, as in blindsight. Neuroscience is not hermetical. If neural typification is even partly informed by correlations with mental types, the prospect of smooth reduction seems far less dim, because the types we are keenest to discover and aptest to select are those that have the right correspondences. Why else all the hubbub about 40-hz oscillations?[7]

But the concern remains that, however we go about specifying neural types, when the dust settles there will still be a plurality of physical types corresponding to any mental type. However, an indefinite disjunction of corresponding physical types could very well *inform* mental typification by suggesting a finer-grained mental typology. Some of these finer-grained mental types might even be distinguishable from a first-person standpoint, such distinctions perhaps being facilitated by the neurological information that suggests them and without which they pass unnoticed, as fine distinctions often do. Even where the finer-grained types are not phenomenologically distinguishable, it is an open question as to whether we have correctly typified the neural types or, if so, whether we might not accept the finer-grained typology anyway, as we could accept it without sacrificing the intrinsic nature of coarse-grained mental types (e.g., pain being intrinsically unpleasant, however we carve up the physical types of pain). Making fine-grained distinctions among familiarly coarse-grained mental types does not obviously compromise the integrity of those types, just as coarse-grained epidermal types are not compromised by much finer-grained epithelial types.

Either the eliminativists are wrong about the reducibility of mental states, or they are right, and it does not matter. This ends the last move-and-counter of the eliminativist gambit. Although I have responded to the moves individually, the whole gambit fails if what I have said about the domain of psychology is correct. Its so-called "failures" fall outside its domain; they are not failures but spotlights on problems certain disciplines, including neuroscience as a *species* of scientific psychology, have yet to solve. Mental states cannot be discounted by the claim, true or not, that they are inadequate for explanatory purposes. Plus, the fact that neuroscience is not hermetical but, rather, is informed by psychology, makes the prospect of smoothly reducing the mental less far-fetched than the Churchlands would have it. This general point is pretty much an aside, however, because the gambit is best met move by move, as above.

"Clever, but they have *got* to be wrong." That is what one thinks after reading an eliminativist manifesto for the first time. I did. Attempts to undermine the mental—consciousness in particular—seem outrageous, or at least ill-motivated. They still do. Denying the existence of experience *as such* flouts common sense without giving it a chance at scientific respectability. Worse, it harbours a misconception of the domain, methods, and status of psychology. Consciousness is not simply part of the explanatory apparatus of folk or scientific psychology, not simply a postulate we can dispense with should better explanations come along. It is something to be explained—and not explained away. That we are far from having an ideal psychology bodes no more ill than the fact that we are far from having a utopian neuroscience, the very prospect for which is prophesied to undermine the mental. If the notion of a utopian neuroscience makes sense at all, the discipline will prove far more accommodating than its otherwise liberal advocates give it credit for.

To ATTACK CONSCIOUSNESS, you do not have to believe in a utopian neuroscience that answers all questions and solves all puzzles. Indeed, seeing utopian neuroscience as a myth can be used as a platform of attack. Significant events in the brain are often a matter of milliseconds. It is often unclear where consciousness fits in the overall picture, or where it begins and ends. The result is that drawing the line *somewhere* seems either procrustean or arbitrary, neither of which is good news to realists. Daniel Dennett speaks to this issue. His elaborate and, in many ways, original view does not so much deny that there is any such thing as consciousness, but that consciousness is not made up of what we think it is. Consciousness, we think, is a matter of what it is like to be the being one is, to have the perspective one has on oneself and the world. The constituents of this perspective are the phenomenal properties of experience, the way this coffee tastes to me now, the way this headache feels, what it is like for me to think the thought of finishing this sentence. These raw constituents of consciousness are called *qualia*, and it is these, not consciousness *per se*, that Dennett targets.

Like the Churchlands, Dennett uses lab reports as grist for his mill, thus gaining a relative advantage over many of his more adversarial colleagues. Unlike the Churchlands, however, he does not always go from lab report to conclusion straight away. He often spins thought-experiments out of what he has gleaned from lab work. A thought-experiment is an imagined scenario invented to test theories, theoretical commitments, and intuitions for conceptual integrity. Dennett calls his thought-experiments "intuition-pumps," the intended connotation being that such scenarios will oust intuitions that stand in the way of clear-sighted theory.

The method of thought-experimentation is important, especially in the philosophy of mind, so I will say a little bit about what it is and what use it has. Take the statement that all artworks must have "significant form." Any artwork we come across that does not have significant form falsifies this general hypothesis. The advantage of thought-experiments is that, in matters of conceptual analysis, you do not need to find actual counterexamples. If I think that significant form is not only necessary but sufficient to count something as art, I can be shown up without anyone going out into the world and finding a non-artwork with significant form. Imagine that the statue *David* was not sculpted by Michelangelo, but occurred freakishly in nature, owing perhaps to a peculiar erosion pattern. It has the same significant form, presumably, but it is not art, its beauty notwithstanding; thus, the hypothesis that anything with significant form is art is falsified. Broadly speaking, thought-experiments help express, sharpen, and test our views when we cannot avail ourselves, in principle or in practice, of tests in the real world.

Out of blindsight, Dennett spins a thought-experiment, which he takes to show that there is effectively no difference between normal vision, which is supposedly qualia-rich, and an idealized case of blindsight, which is not only qualia-poor, but bankrupt. Dennett has us consider a blindsight patient who manages, with the right sort of coaching, to overcome his impairments. Eventually the imagined patient, still devoid of visual qualia, is as adept as normal perceivers in reporting and acting on visual stimuli. There would seem to be no functional difference between the imagined patient and normal perceivers, but, since the imagined patient lacks visual qualia by hypothesis, we have no reason to ascribe qualia to normal perceivers, who are by hypothesis their functional equivalents. The problem is, the imagined patient would not be functionally equivalent to normal perceivers. And if he were, Dennett's scenario would merely dredge up intuitions already at work in other, more familiar thought-experiments.

Dennett's general argument against qualia comes down to this. An entity must make a difference (i.e., have effects in the world) to be quantified over (i.e., count in a list of what the universe contains). All else being equal, the difference between having and lacking qualia, or between having certain qualia and not others, is a difference that makes no difference. So there are no qualia. This argument is contentious, though Dennett distracts attention from this fact by constructing numerous thought-experiments to unhinge the view that qualia do make a difference. Ingenious as these may be, in the end they fail to unhinge the realist position. Even the best among them leaves room for the realist to tell a story no less plausible than Dennett's. Qualia do make a difference-making difference, even in cases where they appear to make none. Although it is perfectly coherent to deny, as many do, the idea that existence implies causal efficacy, that is not the stance I adopt here.

Blindsight patients take themselves to be guessing, taking a stab at the answer, when they discriminate reliably and act skillfully. But this behaviour must be prompted. Verbal stabs are prompted by forcing patients to choose between a pair of provided options. Manual stabs require cueing patients to reach or catch, depending on the task at hand. "What," Dennett asks, "is going on?" Is it "visual perception without consciousness" where the *functions* of vision are still present, but all the good juice of *consciousness* has drained out?"[1] (emphasis in original). Apparently yes, more or less, although the need to give patients cues or options is an important difference between blindsight and normal vision. Unlike patients, normal subjects are spontaneous, confident, and self-sufficient in making perceptual judgments.

To unhinge the notion that there is any "good juice of consciousness" to drain out of normal vision, Dennett constructs a thought-experiment in which, he imagines, the salient (functional) differences between vision and blindsight are removed. The idea is to bring blindsight in line with normal vision by idealizing it out of the functional impairments patients suffer. Suppose that over time and with the right sort of coaching a patient learns to "guess" without prompting. His judgments become increasingly more spontaneous and confident, to the point where he comes to believe what he "guesses" by acts of will. As these "credal willings" become a habit, the patient no longer needs to exercise his will, making judgments as readily and naturally as normal perceivers do. In the end, the patient is a normal perceiver minus the qualia and has not blindsight but *super* blindsight. (Of course this is not strictly true. The imagined patient would lack not only visual qualia but also the brain states by which normal perceivers have them.)

No patients on record have anything like this version of blindsight. They are at a complete loss when left to their own devices, and, although they often improve with practice, taking some time to get up to speed, they fail to show the glimmer of potential to develop such ability. Blindsight seems essentially to depend on at least minimal help in the form of cues or options, except in cases where the relevant options are conceptually decidable (e.g., present/absent) rather than informative (e.g., red/green). Although super blindsight is conceivable, it may not be possible, given natural constraints on visual systems. In other words, it might be logically but not nomologically possible. That is, it might be contradiction-free—it certainly seems to be—but the laws of nature (nomology) might not allow it, in which case super blindsighters would join the rank and file of such fictional entities as zombies and swampmen. (Zombies, imagine, are every bit like us, physically and functionally, except that they lack qualia.)

There is some reason, however, to think that the laws of nature do allow for super blindsight. Patients are already good at detecting whether or not there is a target stimulus in the blind field and, so, in a sense, are able to "guess" when to "guess," even if they need informative disjunctions to "guess" what properties the stimulus has. Monkeys without V1 have something very close to super blindsight. They navigate environments and pick up objects with a facility comparable to that of normal monkeys.[2] Patients might not develop this skill because only part of their visual cortices and corresponding visual fields is destroyed. The intact field is available for most day-to-day visual tasks. In the event that we found a patient whose primary visual cortex was neatly and completely destroyed, we could decide this empirical question. As it stands, at least, super blindsight is not obviously the merely logical possibility that zombies are.

As thought-experiments about consciousness go, super blindsight has the minimal virtue of bringing the issues closer to home. Zombies are harder to imagine, for my part, than super blindsighters. Whether the scenario is nomologically or merely logically possible is beside the point. Neither Dennett's remarks nor my reservations about them depends on one or the other outcome. Consider what Dennett says of the imagined patient, who has acquired super blindsight by some such means as I have described above. He "could treat those stimuli" in the blind field "*on a par* with any conscious experiences. He could think about, and decide upon, policies that hinged on their occurrence as readily as on the occurrence of events consciously experienced"[3] (emphasis added). The idea, again, is to idealize blindsight out of the functional impairments patients suffer, so that although the imagined patient is qualia-bankrupt, he is functionally equivalent to normal perceivers in processing visual information.

The next move is predictable. Since the imagined patient both lacks visual qualia and is functionally equivalent to normal perceivers in processing visual information, we have no more reason to ascribe qualia to normal perceivers than to the imagined patient. And since we deny visual qualia to the imagined patient by hypothesis, ascribing them to normal perceivers is without foundation. One could deny that the imagined patient lacks visual qualia, thus subverting the denial of ascription to normal perceivers. This would be to say, in effect, that we have no *less* reason to ascribe visual qualia to the imagined patient than to normal perceivers. But this is not at all intuitive. Like the story says, the imagined patient starts out a normal patient, devoid of visual qualia in the blind field. Super blindsight does not turn on some inner light but is acquired and exercised in the absence of one.

One could also deny that the imagined patient is the functional equivalent of normal perceivers in processing visual information. There are grounds for this denial. If blindsight is a form of perception at all, it is a quite rudimentary form. Only in simple tasks do patients perform better than chance. They cannot perform higher-order tasks, like perceiving relationships between simultaneous blind field stimuli. Ironically, Dennett fails to mention this, despite his lament that many philosophers overlook elementary facts about the phenomenon. Perhaps the self-sufficiency, spontaneity, and confidence of the imagined patient would correlate with the sorts of higher-order processing beyond the abilities of actual patients. This is not implausible.

Whatever facilitates the imagined patient's quasi-normal perception of simple properties could well facilitate higher-order processing.

For these reasons, I will not follow these lines of rebuttal. Nor will I claim that the imagined patient is a sort of partial zombie that, like the zombie itself, illustrates the epiphenomenal (i.e., non-causal) character of qualia.[4] This would be playing right into Dennett's hands. Instead I want to examine Dennett's contention that in super blind-sight intact and blind field stimuli are on a par. This is plausible, but subtly misleading. The imagined patient's blind field judgments are as readily formed and deployable as his intact field judgments. His handling and management of information in the one field is on a par with his handling and management of information in the other. And both fields contain information—visual information—about visible properties. In this sense, the imagined patient is the functional equivalent of normal perceivers.

However, the fact that the imagined patient is functionally equivalent to normal perceivers in processing visual information does not entail that he is functionally equivalent in all respects. The imagined patient will make the same perceptual judgments about the world, but he will not make the same reports on how he arrived at those judgments. Dennett glosses this distinction, and his thought-experiment turns on this gloss. Consider what the patient would *say* about the two fields. Before the acquisition, he is normal in the intact field and void of visual experience in the blind field. He is mistaken to suppose he can "see" nothing, not that he can *see* nothing. Acquiring super blindsight does not change this, even a little. After the acquisition, the imagined patient either lacks qualia in the blind field altogether, as before, or has another *kind* of qualia, non- or quasi-visual.

Some of my auditory and visual perceptions are roughly at par in Dennett's sense, but I still notice a difference between the way things seem auditorily and the way they seem visually. This is not to say that different sensory modes cannot make things seem the same way. The weather seems stormy whether I see energy discharges in the form of lightning, hear them in the form of thunder, or both. To take a better example, I can tell by sight or by touch that the objects before me (dice) are cubes. This is a convergence of two sensory modes on the way *things* seem, not on the *way* things seem. That I can treat two sets of information on a par does not mean there is no qualitative or even functional difference between them. Just as there is a qualitative and functional difference between convergent perceptions from different sensory modes, so, too, there is a noticeable and reportable difference between vision and super blindsight. If you ask me how I know the objects before me are cubes, my response will depend on how I ascertained that they are—by touch, by sight, or by both. In the same way, the imagined patient will claim to know not by looking but by *blindlooking* that the objects are cubes. And this will be true regardless of whether he lacks qualia in the blind field or has non- or quasi-visual qualia instead. To suppose that he has visual qualia is ruled out by hypothesis.

Dennett's argument against qualia through blindsight thus depends on a subtle equivocation on "the way things seem," a gloss over the distinction between treating sets of information on a par and identifying the manners in which each set is acquired. Smith and Jones may report the same information to their boss, but the boss knows whose report is whose. Even if the imagined patient has qualia in the blind field, he will be non- or at most quasi-visual, and this difference will be both noticeable and reportable. To be a functional equivalent of normal perceivers in processing visual information does not entail functional equivalence overall. Super "seers" are not seers. If the imagined patient were functionally equivalent in processing information *and* in reporting on those processes, he would not have super blindsight but normal vision or, alternatively, "zombiesight." But that is by no means Dennett's scenario. By its own lights, the thought-experiment does nothing to unhinge the realist position.[5]

Of course this might not concern Dennett, as he has a wealth of other intuition-pumps to the same end that do not rely on blindsight. These are too numerous to mention but too important to ignore. Although eliminating qualia is unjustified, I do not claim to have undermined Dennett's overall project. What I do claim to have undermined is his attempt to co-opt blindsight for that project. The difference between super blindsight and normal vision still makes a difference, in the sense that the imagined patient will notice and report phenomenal differences between his blind and sighted fields. Of course, in another sense, it *does not* make a difference, as he is the functional equivalent of normal perceivers in processing visual information. But the point is—or should be—so what?

Over the years, Dennett's arguments against qualia have taken various forms, and he has written about as much on blindsight as any philosopher to date. To my knowledge, he himself came up with the notion of super blindsight as one of his many intuition-pumps, although others have used it for different purposes.[6] Dennett's arguments against the mental generally are presented discursively throughout his work. His attacks on qualia, however, are most concentrated in "Quining Qualia."[7] Like his argument from blindsight, these intuition-pumps are designed to unhinge the view that qualia make a difference-making difference. Whereas the argument from blindsight is meant to show that having or merely lacking qualia makes no difference, these are meant to show that having one or another quale makes none.

Some of Dennett's examples, like his argument from blindsight, gloss over the distinction between the *way* things seem and the way *things* seem. To the untrained ear, an open note on a guitar seems a simple, non-composite sound. But tap the string at the octave fret and the bottom falls out of the note, leaving the harmonic, which the trained ear can tell is a component of the open note. So the sound of the note is not intrinsically simple, contrary to the verdict of the untrained ear. Or consider phenol-thio-urea, which people find either very bitter or completely tasteless. Through eugenics, we could tailor the entire human race to find the substance very bitter or tasteless, and so its taste is not intrinsically one or the other. All this shows, however, is that it is a mistake to think that tasteable things have an actual taste independent of the tongue, or to identify gustatory qualia with some objective property of the thing tasted, even if the former are typically caused by, and may represent, some such property. While the trained ear discerns complexity in the open note through the sound-quale, the untrained ear fails to recognize the complexity through the quale, which itself may or may not be complex. That experts make finer distinctions with the same phenomenal wherewithal does not mean that they, or we, lack that wherewithal.

Many of Dennett's examples play on the distinction between qualia and judgments about them or about the world through them. Several play in particular on the distinction between basic preferences and aesthetic standards, as in the old chestnut: "Hear about the critic who knew art but did not know what he liked?" These examples are meant to show that when one comes to like what one used to dislike, or vice versa, there is no difference between the case where one's experiences have changed in the face of invariant standards and the case where one's standards have changed in the face of invariant qualia. While I am happy to admit the distinction, Dennett's examples would show at most that we should be anti-realists about either qualia *or* aesthetic standards. So much the worse for aesthetic standards, I say. More to the point is Dennett's contention that likes and dislikes are joint products of qualia and standards. You can enjoy experiences without approving of them on some standard, in contradiction to held standards, or without even having standards. Likewise, you can appreciate something on some standard without liking it or without even having an experience of it.

The details of the examples that appeal to aesthetic standards are not particularly important, for Dennett's general point is that when one makes judgments appropriate to certain qualia, there is no difference between having those specific qualia and having others. Imagine we inverted someone's qualia with neurosurgical techniques presently beyond our ken. She sees red instead of green, blue instead of yellow, and vice versa. Or suppose we left the qualia as they are and rerouted all the mnemonic and associative connections to create the same behavioural inversion, as if the qualia had been inverted. No difference, Dennett says. Or suppose we inverted both the qualia and the cognitive links to compensate for the change, such that the two inversions cancelled each other out in the subject's behaviour. According to Dennett, there is no difference between this and the normal case. That is, there is no fact of the matter about what the qualia *really* are.

One is tempted to deny the functional characterization of qualia suggested here, simply because we can imagine cases where *mere* qualia inversion makes no difference. However, when we invert the qualia but not the qualia-judgments, subjects behave as if they have inverted qualia, and this behaviour is evidence for the inversion. But when we invert the judgments but not the qualia, the subject's behaviour is *not* good evidence of qualia inversion, for we know that we have inverted the judgments to mimic the behaviour resulting from genuine qualia inversion. When we do not have an etiology of what has gone wrong, the disjunction of both hypotheses is supported by the subject's anomalous behaviour. But the right etiology rules out one of the disjuncts, and we get the right etiology by default in Dennett's examples, because the behaviour, indicating judgment or qualia inversion, is a result of our deliberate and knowing alteration of the brain areas responsible for qualia *or* judgments about them or about the world through them.[8] Where the etiology is not ours by default, the same neurological knowledge that allows us to create the anomalous behaviour in one of two extremely different ways would allow us to discover in which way the apparent inversion was realized.

Something similar is going on when Dennett has us imagine a machine that could feed one person's experience into someone else's brain, replicating the qualia. Call this machine a transqualiator, or better, a Brainstormer. Imagine that on hooking up two people to the machine, the receiver's behaviour indicates that the sender's qualia are inverted. The grass seems red, the sky yellow, and so on. Then we reverse the polarity on the connector, and the receiver's behaviour indicates normal qualia. The moral we are supposed to draw from this is that since neither polarity is "right," no calibration of the machine canonical, there is no fact of the matter about what the sender's colour qualia really are. One is tempted to say that that is just the point. A functional characterization of qualia fails precisely because the inverted qualia hypothesis is untestable. If we could not tell whether the receiver's normal or inverted set of colour qualia were true to the sender's experience, we would not in fact have a Brainstormer.

But if materialism is true, and qualia are determined by brain states, then however the dependence plays out, it ought to be possible to replicate qualia in phenomenal type. It must be possible to build a Brainstormer. How could we then decide which set of the receiver's qualia was true to the sender's experience? We might insist that whatever fine tuning was required to calibrate the machine, it would be fairly minor, not so open as to allow for polarity, and, hence, qualia, inversions. Notice, though, that the Brainstormer is designed to repli- cate *all* of the sender's experiences, including those from other sen- sory modes, and some of these experiences—taste and hearing, for instance—are conceivably invertible. If, when the receiver's colour qualia are inverted, their taste and sound qualia are normal, this is good evidence that the sender's colour qualia are inverted. If the taste and sound qualia are likewise inverted, where sugar seems salty and high pitches low, then we have good evidence that the connector's polarity is wrong.

Even if these intuition-pumps showed what Dennett thinks they do, they would not suffice to rule out qualia. Ruling them out requires another premise, namely, that only things that make a difference- making difference count. Only causally efficacious entities have a right to existence. This stricture is unduly chauvinistic. First, there is reason to quantify over things like numbers (not countable things, but numbers themselves) and propositions (the meanings of sentences), whose expressions have causal properties, although they themselves do not. Second, it is easy to imagine possible worlds in which there are no causal processes, where many things exist, but nothing makes a difference-making difference. No wonder Dennett focuses on intu- ition-pumps that take attention away from the premise they need to make them work. They stall anyway. Like super blindsight, these other examples leave plenty of room for the realist to tell a better story. Let me put the point succinctly. If Dennett is right, we cannot distinguish blindsight from neglect. But we can. Q.E.D.

I T WOULD HARDLY SEEM NECESSARY to have to argue for the existence of consciousness. To the philosopher of the past, it seemed the only thing an inquiring mind could *not* doubt is that it is conscious. Most of us nowadays are of like mind. But with eliminativism on the table, we cannot take for granted that consciousness exists. In the face of arguments to the contrary, we need to justify the belief in conscious realism. Let me explain this term. If you believe moral properties—like being good and being evil—exist, then you are a moral realist. If you believe that conscious properties—like seeing red or feeling pain—exist, you are a conscious realist. In this chapter, I argue for conscious realism, assembling for the purpose a discursive set of comments from the blindsight literature. We have seen how blindsight has been used, unsuccessfully, in attempts to undermine consciousness. It is time to turn the tables and show how compelling a witness blindsight is, not for the prosecution, but for the defense.

The idea that blindsight supports realism about qualia is not new. As Colin McGinn has said, in blindsight we have "an abnormal case in which the absence of normal consciousness *forces* us to acknowledge its presence in ordinary cases of sight ... as if a biologist had living things brought to her attention by observing the fact of death"[1] (emphasis added). McGinn's analogy here is nice, but somewhat misleading. It is not as though we need unconscious mental processes brought to our attention. As he says, blindsight shows us that visual experience is partly dissociable from visual function and that vision *without* visual consciousness forces us to admit the latter as an ingredient of normal vision. A better analogy, I think, would be "deadlife," where some living functions occur in the absence of genuine life, as in viruses or, if you imagine, self-replicating robots. Unfortunately, McGinn does not explain *how* blindsight forces us to admit conscious realism. In fact, most of the material I will draw on here is likewise underdeveloped, as if it were patently obvious how the admission is forced. It is not. How does blindsight force conscious realism if, as Fodor says, cognitive science is the art of pushing consciousness into a smaller and smaller part of the playing field? Part of the reason is that blindsight helps reveal the neural correlates of consciousness. Because damage to V1 eliminates visual experience but not visual function, V1 is necessary for visual experience, though not for at least some visual function.

My concern in this chapter is not with what the neural correlates of visual qualia are or, primarily, with how we should understand the relationship between qualia and their correlates. My aim instead is to see why the sentiment expressed by McGinn, if true, is true. The blindsight case for consciousness is persuasive, and although part of it points to the causal efficacy of consciousness, my stance, in this chapter at least, is ontologically loaded but theoretically neutral. That is, I want to show how blindsight supports conscious realism without particular attention to which theory of qualia is best. It is not insignificant to note, however, that the best case blindsight makes for realism is also a case for causal efficacy. By focusing on blindsight here, I am not suggesting that realism about qualia is unjustified without it. As a phenomenon salient in recent discussions of consciousness, blindsight fortifies the already strong realist position. This is not only because attempts to undermine qualia through blindsight are unsuccessful, but more importantly because the points on which I will elaborate give realism more real purchase. To see how, I will look at separately motivated observations from John Searle, Philip Cam, Owen Flanagan, and Tim Shallice, to the effect that the world of difference between blindsight and normal vision can be accounted for only by admitting the existence of qualia. Before synthesizing the recast components of the realist case, I will argue for the further, somewhat paradoxical point that blindsight also supports conscious realism because studies of it are themselves investigations of the consciousness conspicuously absent from it.

According to John Searle, "those who doubt the existence of visual experiences" should look at blindsight and "ask themselves what it is that we have that such patients seem to lack."[2] Searle takes his point to be a throwaway, mentioned only in passing. However, it is a substantial point that merits elaboration. Our introspective sense of the difference is that patients lack the visual qualia we enjoy in normal vision, and this requires, in a rather strong sense, that qualia exist. Patients "see" without *seeing*, and part of the normal course of seeing is the enjoyment of visual qualia conspicuously absent in blindsight. The patient's condition is one in which *things* may unconsciously seem certain ways, but for this seeming to be unconscious there must be no *way* in which things seem as they seem. In other words, although there is something it is like to have blindsight, there is nothing it is like to blindsee. Patients are conscious of their condition as one of lacking awareness. Normal perceivers have, while patients lack, a perspective on the stimuli they discriminate, even though both have a perspective on their respective conditions. Perhaps Searle is being cautious when he says patients *seem* to lack qualia, that it is our introspective sense of the contrast that requires conscious realism. Patients really *do* lack qualia, not only because that is our verdict when we imagine the condition, but also because that would be our verdict if we had it. Because patients typically have both blind and intact visual fields, their epistemic situation is better than ours for telling how the two kinds of vision differ phenomenologically. Whereas we imagine the difference, they know it, live it, and report it. Plus, it is very easy to read Searle as challenging the anti-realist to account for the contrast between vision and blindness. The more compelling challenge Searle leaves implicit is to account for the contrast, given that patients seem to have significant rudiments of everything *except* visual consciousness.

Of course there are other ways to contrast the two sorts of vision—for instance, by appeal to the relevant cortical and functional differences. But although V1 is damaged in blindsight, there is still a phenomenal gap that, if left out, leaves the contrast uncaptured. Mere functional differences also fail to capture it. There are cases, as we have seen, where the perceptual judgments of normal perceivers are very much like those of patients in lacking confidence, sophistication, and spontaneity. In these cases, subjects can at least describe what they do see—stimulus background, a fuzzy shape, or whatnot—whereas blindsight patients report no visual experience at all. Even if these other differences explained the phenomenal contrast, they would not explain it away. Eliminativists will harp on the notion that introspection is not infallible, that the contrast, whether imagined by us or experienced by patients, is defeasible, if legitimate at all. Some properties of consciousness are quite unavailable to introspection. You cannot tell simply by having an experience what its neural correlates are. But people typically have substantial authority on the introspectible properties of qualia, and pragmatically speaking, their say-so is all but indefeasible, if subject to refinement by utopian neuroscience and to correction by experts on qualia-based judgments about the world. Despite the limits we may have to place on the authority of introspection, these limits have limits too. Introspection may not be indefeasible, but that is a far cry from the eminently implausible view that first-person reports have no evidentiary weight whatsoever. Even if introspection is fallible, Searle's point, as developed above, is good evidence for the existence of qualia. Perhaps we must buttress this with further evidence, and ideally we should do so, even if we could regard introspection as infallible without raising anyone's hackles. The point is, though, that arguments for the defeasibility of our judgments about qualia do not address the question of whether there *are* qualia.

Suppose that what we think are visual qualia are dispositions to say this or that about the visible world. If so, since patients seem to lack visual qualia, all they really lack are dispositions to say things about the visible world. But patients *do* have such dispositions. They are disposed to say "red" when stimuli are red, "X" when they are X-shaped, and so on. Otherwise they would not *say* "red" when stimuli are red, or "X" when they are X-shaped. Therefore, what we take to be visual qualia simply cannot be dispositions to say this or that about the visible world. Philip Cam says that patients' "often emphatic claims that they do not in any case see the stimuli, coupled with their often reasonably confident discriminations" of stimulus properties, "indicates a world of phenomenological difference between the ordinary subject's experience and that of the subject who is aware only of what he or she is disposed to say."[3] We need to qualify this observation. While patients deny seeing the stimuli they discriminate, their judgments are not at all confident. That is part of the intrigue. Also, it is not entirely clear that patients are immediately aware of their speech dispositions, before the fact, as it were. They take a stab at it when forced, as though they come to know what they are disposed to say only by saying it. Cam's claim, moreover, could simply be read as the complaint that a behaviourist "phenomenology" leaves out qualia. But this claim can be developed into something more substantial. Blindsight pushes a behaviourist "phenomenology" into a position so distorted that it is difficult to see how anyone could find it plausible.

Cam is right to suggest that blindsight poses a keen difficulty for behaviourist "phenomenology." Behaviourism must, by its own lights, explain the difference between blindsight and normal vision in terms of dispositions. But when we take a closer look at the differences, these are few indeed. For instance, patients are disposed to say less sophisticated, less complex things than normal perceivers about visual stimuli, in that they discriminate comparatively simple proper-ties. However many dispositions we add, it seems we are only adding more of the same, more of what is already there; what is decidedly not there is visual qualia. Imagine we had a patient whose blindsight was so good she could discriminate all the visible properties normal per-ceivers do, but only under those conditions in which actual blindsight is exhibited—forced-choice, zero-confidence—a sort of modified super blindsight. We would have no more reason to ascribe qualia to such a patient than to typical patients. All the evidence for not ascrib-ing qualia to typical patients is evidence we would have for denying them to such a patient, so patients' lack of qualia cannot simply be a lack of dispositions that are sufficiently complex. Since patients have a quorum of the right dispositions, the behaviourist must zero in on the one salient difference, that between affirming visual experience and denying it. But whatever plausibility behaviourism might have rests on reducing qualia to clusters of dispositions. To distinguish blindsight by appeal merely to the denial of visual experience fails to distinguish blindsight from hysterical blindness, or simple lying.[4] If qualia are nothing more than dispositions, then there is no difference, from the *patient's* perspective, between blindsight, hysterical blind-ness, and lying. On the flip side, imagine there was a patient who claimed to see what she discriminates, but was otherwise blindsighted—a combination of blindsight and Anton's syndrome. Even without the denials expected of blindsight patients, we would still have all the evidence to corroborate such denials, and so we would have good reason to deny visual qualia *despite* the patient's claims to the contrary. Otherwise the act of asserting that one sees something is a strange kind of utterance on which *really* having seen something magically depends.

The world of difference between blindsight and normal vision cannot be captured solely by appeal to the different dispositions of patients and normal perceivers. Nor do such appeals give us much in the way of explaining the behaviour. To say that someone did something because they were disposed to is vacuous, unless those dispositions are explained in some non-trivial way. But even then the appeal to dispositions contributes little, except to highlight the need for further explanation. True, patients are disposed to deny seeing the stimuli they discriminate, just as they are disposed to "guess" well, but what we want is an explanation of the behaviour itself. For Owen Flanagan, to "explain the observable differences between sighted and blindsighted people," we must "invoke the property of visual consciousness (or lack thereof)."[5] We must, in other words, juxtapose the presence and absence of visual qualia. This point is perhaps less compelling than Searle's, for even if the lack of qualia does not figure in an explanation of blindsight behaviour, our introspective sense of the difference would stand. But the lack of qualia does so figure. Consider the claim of normal perceivers to see and the claim of patients not to see the stimuli they discriminate. Obviously patients are disposed to deny what people normally affirm, namely, that they have visual experience. But why? Is not the best, most natural explanation by appeal to the absence of typically present visual experiences? It is hard to see how else to account for this difference. This is especially clear in super blindsight, where a patient overcomes the functional impairments of blindsight and where the only behavioural difference between the imagined patient and normal subjects is that the patient denies seeing while normal perceivers affirm it. How else could this difference be accounted for? Neurological differences will suffice to explain things like tics and perhaps Tourette's syndrome, because, unlike blindsight, these are not exhibited in consort with the subjects' intentions. Even to explain Tourette's, though, we might need not only a neurological account of the anomaly, but a characterization of the anomaly as producing unintended outputs from the speech-centre.

An account of the neural deficiencies involved in blindsight will not by itself explain the behavioural anomalies of blindsight patients. The absence of certain V1-dependent brain states must be acknowledged as responsible for the lack of perceptual consciousness. The question now is whether we can make sense of the phenomenon, or even describe it well, without admitting the existence of qualia. It may be that all the facts about blindsight can be described without reference to the qualia conspicuously absent from it, but such a description would not be an adequate description *of blindsight*. Tim Shallice says that patients' "phenomenal accounts cannot be ignored" in cases where our interest in phenomena "as pretheoretical generalizations requires them to be couched at least in part in terms of the experience of the subject." A critical aspect of blindsight, for instance, "can only be described in experiential terms."[6] I agree. It is not that we must describe blindsight in terms of patients' experiences, for they have none. We must rather mention the lack of those experiences typical of normal vision, which is likely what Shallice means. Pretheoretical couching is another matter. We can give various accounts of blindsight without mentioning absent qualia, in information-theoretic terms, in terms of the mechanisms of language production involved in reporting tasks, or the motor mechanisms behind action tasks, or some combination of these. Yes, patients' experiential situation is pretheoretically salient, but it is also theoretically salient. Part of what we seek in a psychological theory that accounts for blindsight is an explanation of the relevant psychological phenomena, including not just the performance of patients, or their intact perceptual mechanisms, but such performance *as handicapped by the lack of qualia*. Whatever shape the explanations take, they should account for why patients can perform certain visual tasks even though they lack qualia, because the lack of qualia in blindsight is an inescapable feature of the phenomenon to be explained, not just before but *after* the explanation is had.

Of a piece with Shallice's point, so construed, is this: we cannot make sense of blindsight, we cannot understand it, and, more exactly, we cannot rationalize the behaviour of patients without admitting the existence of qualia. The visual qualia involved in normal vision are part of the conceptual background against which the behaviour of patients can be sensically interpreted. Now, making sense of what someone does usually involves appeal to the intentional states that cause it. Ascribing the right beliefs and desires to me makes sense of what I do, and what I do is good evidence that I have such beliefs and desires. All else being equal, such a belief/desire pair causes me to act the way I do, and the hypothesis that I have that particular pair makes sense of my behaviour insofar as it would be rational, given the belief/desire pair, for me to do what I do. For instance, when, with an unlit cigarette in my mouth, I flick my Zippo, this indicates that I desire to light and smoke the cigarette and that I believe flicking my Zippo is a means to that end, making sense of why I flick my Zippo. The belief/desire pair causes me to flick my Zippo, and it is rational for me to do so because I have that belief and that desire.

I think that qualia serve a similar role in rationalizing behaviour, though perhaps in a somewhat different sense. When, in pain, I say "Ouch!" it is the pain that causes, and makes sense of, my saying "Ouch!" Just as no further explanation is called for when I flick my Zippo, on the hypothesis that I have the above belief/desire pair, no further explanation is called for when I say "Ouch!" on the hypothesis that I am in pain. Although saying "Ouch!" is more or less a reflexive, not an intentional act, it is still rationalizable by appeal to my experience. After all, it would be reasonable to doubt someone who denied pain if they had incurred physical injury and then said "Ouch!" Perception-based action can be rationalized by appealing to a belief/desire pair, but the belief component of such a pair can itself be rationalized by appeal to the qualia from which competent perceivers derive such beliefs. Qualia can rationalize reflexive behaviour directly and intentional behaviour indirectly by making sense of the perceptual beliefs that mediate much of it. To rationalize the emphatic denials of patients that they see anything, we have to deny them the visual qualia that make sense of normal perceivers' perceptual beliefs.

Allowing that patients recognize the difference between blindsight and normal vision—which they do, having both blind and intact fields—requires the existence of those qualia the lack of which is recognized. Of course, it is patients' belief that they have this deficit that rationalizes their behaviour, but it is the lack of qualia that rationalizes this belief.

If we assume blindsight could be adequately described and rationalized without mentioning absent qualia, we would still want to say that it is a visual disorder. Certainly there is physiological evidence to support this conclusion, but it is hard to see how we could claim that blindsight is a visual disorder without being able to avail ourselves of the notion that patients lack qualia. That is the kind of disorder it is. True, patients are less adept than normal perceivers in performing visual tasks and can perform comparatively few tasks. But the fact remains that they are highly reliable in what they do. Without the appeal to absent qualia, we would have to describe blindsight on the order of impairments admitting of degrees, such as nearsightedness and astigmatism. But the condition is not so much a matter of reduced visual function as a dissociation of one kind of vision from another. Those with impaired vision describe what they see, and their degree of function follows. How could we make sense of patients denying that they have visual experience, when, without appeal to absent qualia, we would have no more reason to think of blindsight as a visual disorder than as a bizarre, vision-specific psychosis? With Anton's syndrome, or blindness denial, in which subjects deny *lacking* visual experiences but cannot perform visual tasks, it is unclear whether we have a visual, motor, or cognitive disorder. But the physiological and behavioural evidence make it clear that blindsight is a visual disorder; it is not a matter of neglected visual consciousness. To save its status as a visual disorder, and as the kind of visual disorder it is, is a reductio of the claim that absent qualia are dispensable either in a description of blindsight or in a rationalization of patients' behaviour.

Since blindsight cannot even be described without reference to the visual qualia it conspicuously lacks, such a description will juxtapose blindsight and normal vision. An account of blindsight will inform, furthermore, and, in a certain sense, depend on a theory of normal vision. One should stress why it is reasonable to suppose this. It is reasonable, in part, because the processes underlying blindsight are a limiting case of those subtending normal vision. It is not as though ablation of V1 and the consequent elimination of visual qualia activate some dormant architecture uninvolved in normal vision. As a phenomenon on the fringe of visual phenomena, like other dissociations and like various sorts of illusion, it should come as no surprise that blindsight should have to be described with reference to normal vision and the visual qualia involved in it. Had cold fusion been established as a genuine phenomenon, it would be described with reference to the extreme temperatures involved in normal fusion, as the distinguishing feature of cold fusion would be that it is *cold*, just as the distinguishing feature of blindsight is that it is *blind*. To discover that visual function can occur without qualitative associates is not, however, to marginalize qualia, but rather to stress their significance. Investigations of qualia-independent visual functions do more than subserve theories of normal vision. They are themselves ultimately, if indirectly, investigations *of* visual qualia.

To see how, we have to understand the importance of aberrant visual phenomena to studies of vision. Jerry Fodor states, "Psychologists who have interested themselves in illusions and analogous phenomena have done so" as a "natural consequence of the application of the method of differences to the study of *normal* perception"[7] (emphasis in original). To illustrate this point, Fodor has us consider the following analogy. On most surfaces, water does not bead. That is the normal case, statistically speaking. On especially smooth surfaces, however, water does bead. Why? There are two forces at work—the surface tension of the water and the friction of the surface on which it rests. The surface tension inclines the water toward a spherical shape, while the friction of the resting surface tends to inhibit this action. In the aberrant case, the inhibition is negligible. That is why water beads, when it does. This explanation commits us to a complementary explanation of the normal case, where water does not bead. "In particular," Fodor says, "if the abnormal case is one in which the effects of friction can be discounted, the normal case is simply the one where the effects of friction can *not* be discounted"[8] (emphasis in original).

I do not mean to suggest that Fodor is particularly concerned with consciousness, since he is not, but his remarks are to the purpose. Accounts of aberrant phenomena not only illuminate normal phenomena and suggest certain types of explanation of them, they also *commit* us to certain types of explanation. In blindsight, the effects of visual qualia *have* to be discounted, while normal vision is simply the case where they *cannot* be discounted. Since the behaviour of blindsight patients wants explaining, we do so in part by appeal to their aberrant (absent) phenomenology, which is aberrant only in contrast to the norm, on which its status as aberrant depends. As a description of blindsight has to mention absent qualia, my point is not that we best make such an appeal, but that we *better*.

The raw materials of the blindsight case can now be synthesized into a solid defense of conscious realism. (1) Although there is something it is like to have blindsight, there is nothing it is like to blindsee. The perspectival contrast between blindsight and normal vision requires, in a very strong sense, that qualia exist. (2) The perspectival contrast cannot be captured by a behaviourist "phenomenology," or, for that matter, any other that tries to discount consciousness. (3) The best explanation of the behaviour differences between patients and normal perceivers adverts to the absence and presence, respectively, of visual consciousness. This appeal is strengthened by accounting for the behavioural contrast in terms of neural differences responsible for it and constitutive of the perspectival contrast, a contrast all the more evident in super blindsight—the thought-experiment originally intended to undermine it. (4) The perspectival contrast is not just something we intuit about the phenomenon, but a crucial aspect of the very phenomenon, omissible only by losing its status as the kind of *visual* disorder it is, not to mention the intelligibility of patients' behaviour. (5) Research into blindsight is ultimately research into visual consciousness itself. Having to disregard its effects in the aberrant case that lacks it by definition, we cannot disregard its role in the normal case.

Whatever the particular allegiances of those committed to the existence of qualia, there is something here for everyone. Any conscious realist should be happy with (1), (2), and (4). It is worth noting that the blindsight case for realism is stronger with (3) and (5) than without, and each implies that qualia are causally efficacious. Notice that anti-realists are quick to claim that introspection is at best fallible and, at worst, inadmissible as a means of knowing anything, including what is seemingly so pellucid to it. But however much the introspective basis of (1) is doubted, (2) to (5) fill the gap. Our introspective sense of the difference is compelling, but even more so when it is recognized that consciousness cannot be bought on the cheap and that otherwise we lose not just the best explanation of blindsight, but the very phenomenon that wants explaining.

My stance in this chapter, again, has been ontologically loaded but theoretically neutral. I have tried to emphasize conscious realism while de-emphasizing the fact that its best defense brings with it certain theoretical commitments. I want to stress, again, that the defense of qualia did not have to wait in the wings for a cue from blindsight. Participants on both sides of the debate seem to view the phenomenon as something of a test-case, an *experimentum crucis*. And so, indeed, it is. Conscious realism—imagine the benignly tolerant smile this conclusion would draw from a philosopher of the past, or anyone else, for that matter. But there is no shame in arguing for such a conclusion when it is, in certain quarters, so zealously disputed. For now the defense rests.

ACCESS DENIED, ZOMBIEHEAD REVISITED, AND WHAT MARY DIDN'T THINK SHE KNEW 6

I F A BLINDSIGHT PATIENT is terribly thirsty, and there is a water fountain in their blind field a short way off, what will happen? Nothing. The best explanation of this, according to Owen Flanagan, "is that awareness of the environment facilitates semantic comprehension and adaptive motor actions in creatures like us."[1] Fred Dretske adds, "*that* is a perfectly good answer to questions about what the function of experience is."[2] This is what I call the argument from blindsight, which takes the phenomenon, in which consciousness is conspicuously absent, as a basis for the claim that the absentee has causal efficacy. This sounds reasonable enough. The dysfunction is explained by the lack of consciousness, which by implication is involved, just as we think it is, in the production of thought and action. Reasonable, yes. But straightforward, no. First, there is at least one argument from blindsight *for* epiphenomenalism (the view that qualia are causally inert products of the brain). Second, there are various attempts to block the inference to causal efficacy, keeping epiphenomenalism, for better or worse, a live option. Third, there are some well-known thought-experiments to the effect that, despite the very good reasons we have for thinking that consciousness has causal punch, it really does not, because it *cannot*, and it cannot because we can imagine it not having it. However, even if the arguments for epiphenomenalism can be unhinged, the position itself remains an apparently live option. Can we undermine the position itself, or must we admit that, at most, psychology gives us mere *correlations* between mind and brain?

Some philosophers may have argued that blindsight supports epiphenomenalism; however, I know of no philosopher who has made any such claim in print. The only such argument I do know is by Max Velmans, a psychologist,[3] who argues that a host of dissociation cases including blindsight, as well as many of those discussed earlier, shows that qualia are not necessary for a significant range of information processing. Hence, the amount of information processing performable without *any* conscious concomitant marginalizes the causal role of qualia—right to the margin, in fact. Qualia are, in effect, epiphenomenal.

There are at least two things wrong with this argument. First, although qualia are not necessary for certain sorts of anomalous visual processing, it does not follow that they are not involved in normal perception. Nor does it point to their having a marginal role, much less no role whatsoever, in a broad band of mental activity. True enough, patients are capable of a substantial amount of visual processing and perform well on a significant range of visual tasks. But of equal importance is the fact that they are incapable of doing many things normal perceivers can, such as performing more sophisticated sorts of processing and doing so without cues or options. Qualia are not necessary for what patients *can* do. Does not this suggest that they are necessary for what patients *cannot* do? Even if qualia were not necessary for what patients cannot do, it still would not follow that they are not involved in normal vision. However much cases like blindsight might seem to push qualia towards the margin, they do not—and it seems they never could—push them right *to* the margin. If we had a super blindsighter, who lacked qualia but was otherwise the functional equivalent of normal perceivers, this would show only that qualia are not necessary for full "visual" function, not that they play no part—even a leading role—in normal vision. It would not be strictly true that such a patient had full visual function, for they would still deny having qualia, and having qualia at all is an important part of normal vision. To see this, imagine we had a subject who was completely super blindsensed, having super blindsight throughout the visual field, blindtouch throughout the tactile field, and so on. Such a subject would not be able to tell that certain information—which might have been acquired through other senses—is *visual*, because qualia are the means for determining by what sensory mode information is acquired. The super blindsighter knows by subtraction that blindseen information is visual.

So what exactly is wrong with inferring the causal efficacy of consciousness from blindsight? According to Ned Block, the problem is this: "conscious" has different senses. There is phenomenal consciousness, which consists in qualia, the sense of the term we have been meaning all along. But there is also "access" consciousness, which is possessing and being able to deploy information—a kind of consciousness, Block says, we might and perhaps should ascribe to zombies.[4] Access consciousness seems to be a kind of informational sensitivity. Do not blindsight patients have that, and do they not, then, have at least some measure of access consciousness? No, Block says, because they cannot deploy information spontaneously. They need cues. If they did spontaneously deploy information—if, that is, they had super blindsight—then they would have access consciousness. Access consciousness, then, is something like informational sensitivity plus spontaneity. The inference to causal efficacy of phenomenal consciousness does not work, supposedly, because patients lack both kinds of consciousness. For all we know, it may be the lack of access that is to blame. Notice that, if Block is right, we can still infer the causal efficacy of consciousness in *some* sense. The lack of qualia may be to blame, or the lack of access, or both. It is one of the two, at least. But that is petty consolation. It is the qualia we care about.

Trouble is, it is not at all clear that we should be inclined to call this other form of consciousness consciousness at all. Why not? Access consciousness is peculiar. Is there any sense in which we should ascribe consciousness to zombies? Indeed, given the nature of this term of art, is there any sense in which we *can* ascribe consciousness to zombies?—they are supposed to be unconscious automata. How can we pull access away from qualia when, in the real world, as Block admits, they always go hand in hand? That is why Block appeals to the imaginary case of super blindsight for illustrative purposes. If access goes hand in hand with qualia in the real world, this means not that access is another kind of consciousness, but that it is evidence *for* consciousness in the normal, phenomenal sense. Indeed, lack of access is part of the reason we deny patients phenomenal consciousness. What would it mean to say that information is available to me but, despite this, it is something of which I am unconscious in the normal sense? Some of my memories are unconscious. They are retrievable using the right search procedures and so are available in that sense. But they are *potentially* conscious, not conscious in some other way. When they are poised for use—that is, when I have retrieved them—I am phenomenally conscious of them. As a sort of informational availability, access consciousness is fundamentally ambiguous. It either means informational sensitivity, which patients have, and is not a form of consciousness, or it is a criterion of consciousness in the normal sense.

In what other ways might one try to block the inference to causal efficacy? Well, one might turn skeptical about the thing to be explained. David Chalmers, for instance, adopts this strategy by saying that our description of blindsight is underdetermined by the data. In other words, we do not know enough about what blindsight is to be sure of what conclusions may be drawn from it. Up to this point, we have understood blindsight as a species of vision without visual consciousness. But, Chalmers claims, we cannot rule out the possibility that patients have a faint sort of experience, one that maybe "bears an unusual relation to a verbal report."[5] Because it is not clear that visual function and qualia come apart in blindsight, no argument assuming otherwise is warranted. Of course, even if we cannot rule out the possibility of faint, unrecognized experiences, the inference to the causal efficacy of the *missing* consciousness still goes through.

Let us assume that, if blindsight is underdetermined in the sense Chalmers intends, no metaphysical conclusions follow. No matter, because blindsight is not underdetermined in the sense Chalmers intends. The idea of a faint quale that bears an unusual relation to a verbal report is rather vague. What kind of relation is it? Similarity? Unconscious cause? It would be strange to posit a type of visual experience so faint as to be mistaken for a verbal report or for the kind of thought normally expressed by such reports. It is strange already to posit a type of visual experience of which the subject is unaware either as an experience or as visual. This would mean that there is a kind of consciousness the essential feature of which is that it is inaccessible to consciousness, a notion which I have already discarded. Again, there are cases where patients report a faint experience or a vague feeling of awareness, and these are distinguishable from full-fledged blindsight, since patients notice and report them *as* faint qualia and because patients sometimes perform *worse* with such residua than with a complete phenomenal void.[6] The indeterminacy Chalmers worries about is not only conceptually problematic, it is empirically false.

Another, more basic strategy is to deny that the alleged best explanation is best. On this view, an equally good, if not better explanation of blindsight is that patients lack the brain states on which epiphenomenal qualia depend. Such an account might be equally consistent with the data, but that does not mean it is an equally good explanation. Causal efficacy is much more plausible from a commonsense point of view or from an introspective stance. Consciousness seems involved in producing thoughts and actions. That patients lack qualia explains not only their handicapped perception, but why, despite their good performance, they insist on lacking qualia. Assuming that blindsight points to some species of "naturalism," where qualia stuff is *some* sort of physical stuff, however defined, this has the added virtue of being simpler than the epiphenomenalist alternative. Qualia are part of the physical world, not inexplicable onlookers that hang above it. If so, this view has the further virtue of cohering better with our stock of empirical knowledge. Moreover, if we accept that the anomalous case of blindsight is one in which the effects of qualia have to be discounted, this, as we saw earlier, commits us to saying that normal vision is a case in which such effects cannot be discounted. For such reasons, the causal efficacy of qualia is part of a better explanation of blindsight than the epiphenomenalist alternative. Still, it might be that the principled arguments for epiphenomenalism would force us to concede the point. It is time, then, to turn to epiphenomenalism's best friends, zombies and Mary.

Zombies are identical to us in every way but one—they have no qualia. They are exact physical replicas of their conscious counterparts, atom for atom, molecule for molecule, property for property, process for process, and yet are mere automata. The fact that we can imagine zombies is supposed to show that consciousness has no causal punch. If the zombiephile is right, then it does not matter that ascribing causal efficacy to qualia is part of the best explanation of blindsight and of human behaviour generally. Best is not good enough. How does the argument work? By taking three things for granted.

First, it takes for granted that zombies are conceivable, that we can, in fact, imagine them. Their conceivability is taken, second, to imply their possibility. Third, this possibility is taken to have purchase on natural law in such a way that qualia cannot have causal efficacy. There are two important senses of the term "possibility" here. A logically possible scenario is one conceivable without contradiction. A naturally possible scenario is one compatible with the laws of nature. The causal efficacy of consciousness rules out the natural possibility of zombies, so if zombies are naturally possible, then consciousness is not causally efficacious.

Zombies can be neutralized, in philosophy as in horror films. The key is to avoid taking for granted what the argument requires. We might claim that zombies are not, in fact, conceivable. As far as I am concerned, it is difficult to imagine them. Exact physical replication is all the evidence we could ever have for, and all we could ever mean by, phenomenal identity, in which case the very notion of zombies is incoherent and not even a logical possibility. This might be true even if zombies are conceivable, as they seem to be. Suppose I told you that Peano arithmetic might be both consistent and complete. This seems conceivable enough, but Gödel's proof shows, *as a matter of logic*, that it cannot possibly be both. Conceivability is not, then, a trustworthy guide to logical possibility. I am perfectly willing to concede, as do most philosophers, that zombies are both conceivable and logically possible. But this concession is less straightforward than it is often taken to be and is of little avail besides. The logical possibility of zombies does not tell us anything—much less anything interesting— about the status of qualia in naturally possible worlds like ours. After all, it does not falsify epiphenomenalism to imagine a world in which consciousness is *not* epiphenomenal. No, what the true-blue zombiephile needs is natural possibility, but that is established by testing in one way or another, and zombies, being fictional constructs, cannot be revealed by any kind of test.

That the logical possibility of zombies should rule out the causal efficacy of qualia is patently implausible. But let us assume otherwise and do a reductio. If zombies play havoc with natural consciousness, this throws, on pain of inconsistency, the whole natural order out of whack. Water is not H_2O, because I can imagine that it is CH_4. Epidermal properties are not epitheleal properties, for I can imagine my skin, not as composed of epitheleal cells, but as one giant proto-plasmic sheet. Planetary orbits cannot be elliptical, because I can con-ceive of them as circles with epicycles. The epiphenomenalist might complain that these analogies do not work. In my examples, I am imagining changes in lower-level properties, not higher-level proper-ties. Plus, in my cases, I am imagining a change, not an absence. An imagined change is not an imagined absence. In response, let me say, first, that the relative level of properties imagined is not crucial to my point, nor that my examples are about imagined changes rather than imagined absences. I can imagine that H_2O is invisible in solid, liquid, or gas form, that epitheleal cells produce no higher-level epidermal properties, or that the planets are unobservable, like dark matter. If the complaint is now that these are inconceivable, it should be recalled who set the bar for conceivables so low in the first place. If the complaint is that conceivables only count when the status of the mental is at stake, it is hard to see why the scope of application should be so limited. The only reason is to rule qualia out of the causal order without having to make similar rulings elsewhere. And that is unfair.

Another familiar thought-experiment concerns the utopian neu-rologist Mary. Mary, we imagine, knows everything there is to know from a third-person perspective about colour vision and yet has never experienced colour. She is kept in a colourless room, observing the world through black-and-white monitors. Or she is colourblind or has special glasses that filter out colour. The mechanics do not really matter. She knows positively everything about surface reflectance, wave transmission, retinal absorption, how the brain processes colour information and yields colour experiences, how these affect cogni-tion—everything. She knows a great deal about colour experiences, but she has never had them herself. Now, imagine that Mary comes out of the room (or has her colourblindess corrected or her filter glasses removed) and has the inaugural colour experience of seeing a ripe tomato. "Oh," she says, "*that's* what it is like to see red." The intended intuition here is that, even with otherwise complete knowl-edge of colour vision (i.e., complete physical knowledge), on seeing red she learns something new about a certain kind of colour quale—what it is like to have it. The intended moral is that qualia are not physical but epiphenomenal, since there is more information to be had about qualia than complete physical information.[7]

There are various replies that can be made here to avoid the epiphenomenalist moral. First, we might object that, if Mary comes to learn something by seeing the tomato, she could not have had complete knowledge of colour vision, even from a third-person perspective. Or, we might claim that, since Mary knows all the physical facts, she has to know in *some* sense what it is like to see red, even before seeing the tomato. Such replies may seem to beg the question, for they suggest that the thought-experiment is incoherent as described. However, it is not obvious that the scenario is coherent, in part because the notion of complete but *pure* physical knowledge is radically unclear. Would Mary know general facts, particular facts, or both? Would she know that her physical knowledge was complete? It may not seem to matter, so long as we deny her previous colour experience. But if Mary's previous knowledge, as we conceive it, is that vague, it seems we cannot rule out that the experience she lacks is *necessary* for the knowledge we assume she has.

One of the more standard replies is to admit that Mary acquires "something knowledge-related" but deny that she acquires anything besides the trivial knowledge that she is seeing red *now*. What she acquires is a new *way* of knowing what she already knew or a new ability to recognize red by phenomenal redness. Consider Russell's distinction between knowledge by description and knowledge by acquaintance. Part of the point of this distinction is that one can have knowledge of things one has never experienced. Failing direct experience, a fact can be known by justified inference to the appropriate description.[8] The nature of such inferences is unimportant here, for we allow that Mary knows all relevant facts of the form "Subject S has quale Q." She has never been a Q having S before, but she already knows by description all the facts about S's having Q's, as could, in principle, someone who was blind or had "20/20 blindsight." This way of understanding qualia was recommended by Herbert Feigl, long after Russell proposed the distinction and, ironically, long before

Mary's debut.[9] It is both unfortunate and surprising that in connection with this thought-experiment, where his work seems especially germane, Feigl is mentioned not at all or as a mere historical curiosity. He deserves better.

Of course it is precisely the intrinsic nature of phenomenal redness that the epiphenomenalist insists that Mary comes to know only by seeing the red tomato. In other words, the epiphenomenalist claims that qualia can be known by acquaintance only, that what is known essentially through experience is unknowable by description. And so, in addition to all the physical facts about colour vision, there are further facts about what it is like to be a colour-seeing subject. One such fact is what Mary comes to know through her inaugural colour quale—that seeing red is like *this*. But even if Mary comes to learn what it is like to see red, this does not add anything to her universal inventory, her catalogue of what there is. She already includes qualia. Knowing a good deal about them, she has to. She knows that a quale Q must be experienced by some subject S, that Q lasts only so long as it is experienced by S, that being the S that has the Q means being in brain state B, and so on. Epiphenomenalism follows only if what one has acquaintance with when one has qualia are not physical properties, the latter being essentially knowable only by description. We are not always right about essential properties, however. First-hand knowledge of the colour of something might seem to depend essentially on having the right experience, but blindsight patients have such knowledge in the absence of any experience at all. Moreover, to insist that physical properties cannot be known the way qualia are is to beg the question against materialism.

So the thought-experiment does not really turn on whether a case can be made for the claim that Mary knows what it is like to see red despite never having had the pleasure. Even so, I want to suggest that she does know what it is like, even before her inaugural quale. On seeing red at first, Mary says, "Oh, *that's* what it is like." She is not surprised that she has the quale, although, admittedly, she could not have imagined what it would be like. Nonetheless, she *recognizes* it, both as a colour quale and as the colour quale it is. Her recognition (note the etymology: re-cognition) is at least good evidence that she already knew what it is like to see red even though she could not have known that she did. Regardless of what causes the quale, be it a ripe tomato, a diffused light, or a patch of paint, Mary will recognize her inaugural quale.[10] Why? Again, it is hard to imagine what it means to have complete, pure physical knowledge, and so it is not obvious that Mary would lack this recognitional ability. Indeed, so long as we deny her previous colour qualia, we seem free to allow Mary anything that does not contradict this, including the ability to recognize her inaugural quale. We can often recognize things we have not experienced, if we know the appropriate descriptions. Believe it or not, when I first saw chartreuse, I recognized it right away. A friend had described it as "the most emetic shade of green imaginable," not that I could have imagined it. More importantly, since Mary knows she is in brain state B, and since she already knew that having B is sufficient for having Q, she *must* be able to identify her inaugural quale. Although her identification will be a matter of inference, it is important to realize that *all* recognition is inferential. Recognizing something via memory is no less an inference than recognizing something via perspicuous description.

So the zombies are dead, and Mary is quite contrary to her intended purpose. The standard replies are, I think, conclusive, but I hope to have added to them in at least a somewhat provocative way. Nonetheless, having unhinged some of the major arguments for epiphenomenalism, we have not ruled it out. The best explanation of blindsight will advert to the causal efficacy of qualia, but the epiphenomenalist suspicion lingers on. Whatever successes the materialist program has, however many mind/brain correlations we get, it is always open to the epiphenomenalist to say that mere correlations are all we ever get. Visual qualia are correlated with V1-dependent brain states and are perhaps dependent on them *as* epiphenomena.

This "mere correlations" fallback deserves further scrutiny. Assume, as almost everyone in the debate now does, that the physical world is causally closed. To say that qualia have neural correlates, then, is to say that (1) qualia depend on those brain states and (2) that they occur at the same time as those brain states. The dependence is either causal or non-causal. If it is causal—that is, if the brain states cause the qualia—we have a bit of a quandary. How could qualia be the effects of brain states if they themselves have no further effects? There is no such thing as the last link in a causal chain, except perhaps at the end of time, and we are not there yet. In addition, causes precede their effects, and so we lose the temporal correlation. While, in physics, there seem to be cases of effects which are simultaneous with their causes—the photoelectric effect, for instance—the effect, such as a flash of light, tends to be of the same kind as the cause, and it is only because of the verification of such phenomena that they present any challenge to the ordinary concept of cause-and-effect. Epiphenomenal qualia miss on both counts. On the other hand, if the dependence is non-causal, what kind of dependence is it? There are two ways out of this explanatory nightmare. We can go back to causal dependence, which does not work, or go forward to materialism, which gives a straightforward explanation of non-causal dependence.

There is a further problem with the "mere correlations" fallback. How do we know that visual experience typically precedes visual belief, as when I see a yellow cab, I then come to believe that there is a yellow cab in front of me? I remember as much from many past experiences. On the epiphenomenalist view of things, my mnemonic experience is in no way affected by the experiences I seem to remember. Maybe my memory systematically gets things backwards. That is silly, no? Memory is, if nothing else, reliable. How can this be if epiphenomenalism is true, and the experiences which are later remembered are not in any way involved in the formation of the memory? The brain states on which my memories depend must be *faithful* to past experience. This means that the neural correlates of the experience must contain and pass on the relevant information. This includes information about what it is like to have those experiences, and the whole point of epiphenomenalism is that such information *cannot* be contained in something objectively accessible, such as a brain state. And if brain states can contain what-it-is-like information, they can just as well be qualia, which makes epiphenomenal qualia redundant. More importantly, though, it means this: if epiphenomenalism is true, it is false. Therefore, it is false.

A THEORY THAT BEST EXPLAINS a phenomenon, or set of phenomena, is worth endorsing for that reason. All else being equal, a theory is best if it is simplest, most testable, explains the most phenomena, or coheres best with the rest of our body of knowledge. Sometimes it is clear when an explanation is best; yet, although philosophy is continuous with science in important respects, this is more often the case with scientific theories. In philosophy, especially, it can be difficult to discern which explanation is best because an explanation that seems best for reasons of simplicity or coherence (with other knowledge) might be objected to more readily than in science on *principled* grounds (i.e., on grounds of simple coherence). The epiphenomenalist does not object to materialism on the grounds that it is not a simple, elegant account of how mental states can be causally efficacious in a world of physical causes. The epiphenomenalist cites principled reasons why mental states simply cannot be physical states, despite our introspective sense that they have causal powers and despite the explanatory virtues of ascribing them. Arguments to the effect that qualia are causally efficacious will have to incur such principled objections. Some of these were dispatched in the last chapter, but there are certain others to contend with.

We find arguments from best explanation in many spheres of philosophy, often, though not always, to establish the existence of certain kinds of entity that are, in one sense or another, unobservable. The classic case often used to illustrate the importance of best explanation is the inference from such observable phenomena as vapor trails in cloud chambers to the existence of certain subatomic particles which cause them. We admit the existence of subatomic particles because they are part of the best explanation of various phenomena, including vapor trails in cloud chambers. In the theory of knowledge, it is argued that the best explanation of how a belief can be justified is that it is itself the product of an inference to the best explanation. Some moral philosophers argue that certain behaviour patterns are best explained by appeal to the agent's moral character. Some philosophers of mind hold that behaviour is best explained by appeal to the agent's brain states *as* identified with those mental states that rationalize the behaviour. I will not linger on the relative merits of these arguments, although it should be noted that they are not all equally plausible. It is hardly clear, for instance, that all instances of knowledge are the product of inferences, much less inferences to the best explanation. Nor is it my purpose to examine in detail the nature of best explanation, the composite theoretical virtues it relies on, or even the relative importance of these virtues. I avoid this not just because these are matters of some dispute, but because my principal aim in this chapter is to explore the implications of the last chapter.

Consciousness does not only matter, it makes a difference. It has causal powers and is involved, more or less as we think it is, in the production of thought and action. We can say this because ascribing causal powers is part of the best explanation, not just of normal human behaviour, but of such aberrant phenomena as blindsight. But how is it that qualia have such causal powers? What is the best explanation of that? You might be tempted to think that the best explanation is simply—in both senses of "simply"—materialism. Mental states are brain states. What could be better than that? Indeed, best explanation arguments first emerged in the philosophy of mind in service of precisely that agenda. However, almost no one in the philosophy of mind accepts simple materialism. There are two reasons why. First, and less importantly, there is the lingering dualist suspicion that mental states cannot be brain states but, instead, must inhere in a non-physical substance of some kind. Second, and more importantly, there is the idea that any type of mental state—being in pain, say—can be realized in more than one physical way. Being in pain is produced not by any single type of brain state, but by a plurality of such types and perhaps by other, non-neural physical states besides. This means that mental states do not map onto physical states one-to-one, as the more traditional brands of materialism require. The correspondence is rather one-to-many. It is for this reason, especially, that the more traditional brands of materialism are presumed dead. However, despite widespread acceptance and seeming inevitability of the one-to-many picture of mental mapping, not to mention what are taken to be the implications of this picture, it is the traditional sort of materialism that I will defend here. Let us tackle the dualist suspicion first.

In its contemporary guises, the dualist suspicion comes up in a variety of complex arguments, most of which find inspiration and guidance in a particular argument by Saul Kripke.[1] The objection is rhetorically clever and Cartesian in flavour, with a semantic twist. At its heart is a disanalogy between pain and temperature. Kripke grants that, just as [temperature = mean kinetic energy], there may be a single, neural x such that [pain = x]. In other words, we could have the same type relations between pain states and brain states that we have between heat and its microphysical correlates. For the identities to be true, Kripke argues, they have to be necessarily true, not just true as a matter of natural law, but true as a matter of natural law in such a way that we cannot imagine them false. This may seem to be a strange requirement, especially as Kripke admits that there are senses in which both identities are imaginably false, and yet, while he aims to undermine the pain equation, he also aims, wisely, to preserve the heat equation. The objection turns on explaining away the imaginable falsity of the heat equation in a way that cannot explain away the imaginable falsity of the pain equation. You can feel heat in the absence of real heat, and you can also fail to feel heat in the presence of real heat. But you cannot feel pain in the absence of real pain or fail to feel pain in the presence of real pain. When we imagine the heat equation false, we are mistaking felt heat for real heat, yet when we do the same for pain we cannot be mistaking felt pain for real pain. Felt pain *is* real pain.

Suppose we admit that heat and pain are disanalogous in this way. The disanalogy only does the work it is supposed to do if the heat equation is imaginably false only when we confuse felt heat for real heat, or if other physical identities are imaginably false by such a confusion alone. However, I can imagine that thermometers register ultraviolet light, or radiation, or something else besides the micro-correlates of temperature. Conversely, I can imagine that the micro-correlates of temperature constitute something besides temperature, such as a sonic inhibitor property. Here, too, it seems we skirt the felt/real confusion without sacrificing imaginability. The predictable sort of reply is this: the meaning of "temperature" as used by physicists and other experts *guarantees* that these failed identities are in no sense imaginable. I doubt the experts would agree. But if it were true regardless, then this only goes to show that our expertise in matters of mind simply is not yet developed enough to "guarantee" the same for psychophysical identity. We are not even confident yet about what the neural correlates of consciousness are, nor have such hypotheses been ramified as scientific fact. In the event that we acquire such knowledge, there would be no reason why the pain equation should be any less of a guarantee.

The dualist suspicion is rooted in Descartes' way of thinking about the relationship between mind and brain. A conscious state seems radically different from what a neuroscientist could have access to—a brain state. Of course, it does not follow from the fact that the two *appear* different that they *are* in fact different, but the suspicion lingers. Kripke's objection reflects these more general misgivings that people tend to have about materialism. How could qualia, which are seemingly so different from brain states, *be* brain states? Consider an analogous question. How could mass, which is seemingly so different from energy, *be* energy? That a proposed identity appears radically implausible at first glance is no serious mark against it. Mass/energy identity is no less astonishing than mind/brain identity. Yet while the former is clearly acceptable, proponents of the dualist suspicion frame the latter as a unique case where intuitions as old as Descartes have executive authority. However, there is no possible world in which you can have your cake and eat it too.

The second objection is much more involved, and I will devote the rest of this chapter to answering it. Materialism, in its classical form, is reductive. It implies that for any type of mental state, there is only one type of physical state to which it corresponds. Mental types correspond to physical types one-to-one, and each mental type is identical to, thus reduced to, its physical correspondent. The objection is that, for mental types, there probably or principally can be no such univocal physical correspondence.[2] The correspondence is one-to-many rather than one-to-one, because for any type of mental state, there is more than one physical type of realization. If my pain right now maps onto a certain brain state, a different type of brain state may do the same thing and feel the same way on another occasion. Although any instance of pain will be identical to a brain state of some particular type, being in pain generally will map onto a plurality of such types. There will be no single brain state B_1 such that [pain = B_1]. The equation will rather look like [pain = B_1, or B_2, or B_3, or ...]. It will be, in other words, disjunctive. But reduction requires that the x in [pain = x] be non-disjunctive, because disjunctive properties do not enter into laws, and successful reduction preserves laws. Mental states, then, cannot be brain states in the sense that reduction requires. The failure of type identity leaves two options. One is functionalism, which identifies mental states with the job a physical state has to do—the causal role it must play, the function it must serve—if it is to be part of the appropriate disjunction. Another option is non-reductive materialism, which accepts the one-to-many picture of mental mapping, but rejects functionalism along with type identity.

Functionalism is often objected to on the grounds that it cannot handle cases of qualia inversion, where we imagine that the functional specifications of a subject's visual system remain intact while, to the subject, grass appears red, the sky yellow, and so on. The complaint is that functionalism leaves out the intrinsic nature of qualia in a way that other species of naturalism do not. It might be insisted that qualia have no intrinsic nature apart from their functions, or that intrinsic differences at least imply functional differences. But here we are dealing with mere conceivables, and so it is hard to see whether qualia are invertible in any interesting sense or, if so, what follows. In the argument from blindsight, we assign qualia some of the functions performed by normal but not by blindsight visual systems, including those that account for normal perceivers' claims to having visual experience. Qualia are whatever perform those functions, but this is not to say that qualia are *merely* the performance of those functions. To claim the contrary would be to offer explanations seemingly as trivial as those offered by behaviourism. Compare "The computer did that because that is its function" with "He did that because he was disposed to." The V1-dependent states, which are absent in blindsight and which help explain why patients deny seeing anything, are trivial when defined by their functional properties, but not when defined otherwise. Their location or distribution in the brain, their microstructure, and the intrinsic nature of their qualial correlates are all related to functional properties in important ways, but not equivalent to them. Just as the behaviour of glass is explained by its physical properties, the behaviour of blindsight patients is explained by the physical properties of the qualia they lack. To figure into informative explanations, qualia cannot be specified in purely functional terms.

It seems, then, that we are left with token identity. Many philosophers are resigned to it and work hard to develop satisfactory versions of non-reductive materialism. Non-reductive materialism has its share of problems, though. First, it does not anchor the mind to the physical world in the way we should ideally want, and this opens a door to many arguments, both simple and sophisticated, for epiphenomenalism and, yes, eliminativism. Consider, for instance, that if [pain = B_1, or B_2, or B_3, or ...], then it is the Bs that really count, for it is they alone that participate in the causal nexus. While any particular pain will be identical to one of the Bs, since it is the Bs as *Bs* that have causal powers, nothing about a B being a pain matters. So we lose, not mental causation *per se*, but the kind of mental causation worth wanting, where pains are caused the way they are, and have the effects they do, because they are *pains*. I will not dwell, here, on the pitfalls of token identity. My strategy is somewhat different. I want to focus on the idea of one-to-many mapping. Non-reductive materialism is, at core, a twofold view. First, the mental maps one-to-many onto physical properties. Second, as a consequence of this mapping, while particular mental states are physical, mental properties are not. I argue, in defense of type identity, against both these commitments.

Why should we believe that mental states are multiply realizable, that they map onto brain states one-to-many rather than one-to-one? Maybe the one-to-many mapping picture has been too hastily drawn. How much variation is there in the neural realization of mental states?

Owen Flanagan, for instance, avows a sympathy for type identity as "a first and rough approximation," but two not uncommon misgivings steer him away from full endorsement.[3] One concern is that only some qualia, like those of colour, seem to map neatly onto neural types. Others, like pain, do not. If so, then while pain seems to count as a loss for type identity, colour qualia count as a victory. But what about pain? I made a suggestion earlier to the effect that a disjunctive set of corresponding physical types could motivate a finer-grained mental typology, which is entirely plausible in the case of pain. Any paint store has swatches of hundreds of colours, but how many types of pain do we bother to distinguish? I assume that a difference in the felt location of a pain does not imply a difference in pain type, just as a difference in location of a colour in the visual field does not imply a difference in phenomenal hue. We probably need a finer-grained typology for pain to account for certain pain-related phenomena, its susceptibility to willful control, variations in endurance thresholds, the pleasurable pain of masochism, and the like. While we distinguish sharp pains from throbbing pains and so on, there are probably other phenomenological distinctions that we could make, but do not, because it is not worth developing the sort of discriminative expertise you find in other domains of experience, such as wine-tasting. The pain and getting rid of it are what matter, not becoming a connoisseur of pain. We may also be motivated to adopt finer-grained typologies for pain even if such distinctions are not phenomenologically distinct. Given the variety of pain-related phenomena, it seems possible that some forms of pain are unlike many other qualia in being cognitively penetrable, that is, influenced by the subject's beliefs and desires, although other forms, like pain "in" phantom limbs, seem quite the opposite. Such influence may explain the proliferation of physical pain types and, if controlled for, dispel it. Allowing either this or a finer-grained typology for pain could seemingly account for the rough correspondence that worries Flanagan.

Besides finer-grained mental typologies and accounts of cognitive influence, there are other strategies to employ in avoiding the one-to-many mapping picture. For the neural correlates [B_1, or B_2, or B_3, or ...] of any mental type, a B must play the right functional role for it to count in the disjunction. It is not clear, however, that this is the only thing a B has to have. Since some qualial types do seem one-to-one mappable, others may not, simply because we do not yet have the right neural typology. Perhaps, on this yet unavailable neural typology, there is some non-functional property P such that each of the Bs in [pain = B_1, or B_2, or B_3, or ...] is also a B_p. In fact, the most natural explanation of why each of the Bs plays the same functional role is that it shares a common structural property. Different neurons or neuronal groups may exhibit this property at different times or in different individuals, but so long as the right structural *pattern* is exhibited, the variation will not matter. Let me explain. You see a vertical pattern of black and white stripes when selective neurons fire in corresponding *columns* in your brain. However plastic or otherwise variable brains might be, this suggests that perceptual qualia and mental states generally have their own distinctive neural patterns. If such patterns run the gamut of the Bs in a one-to-many mapping, a one-to-one mapping falls out. Indeed, without the Bs having some such structural commonalities, not only does their shared functional role become mysterious, non-reductive materialism seems open to the very same objections that hamstring functionalism.

Even if we had one-to-one mapping onto *brain* states, this by itself would not do, for various non-neural states may do the job just as well. If a robot could feel pain, for instance, its pain would be a silicon state, not a brain state.[4] This might seem a bit far-fetched, but consider a simpler case. Suppose we developed a silicon "painmaker," the purpose of which is to correct the neurological deficit of people who cannot feel pain. We cannot yet make a painmaker, but it is a distinct possibility that we may one day be able to do so. We are already developing the technology to replace damaged neuronal groups. If silicon painmakers could both function and feel like ordinary pain, which is correlated not with silicon states but with a certain brain state (likely thalamic), then pain cannot be identified with that brain state. Consider the following analogies, however. Artificial hearts might function like ordinary hearts and may even feel the same to those that have them. For an amputee, a prosthesis functions in important respects like the missing limb. Otherwise it would not be a prosthesis. A perfect prosthesis would function like an ordinary limb and feel just the same. As with painmakers, synthetic hearts and limbs can function and feel like the real thing. What is the point of these analogies? Simply this: artificial hearts are not hearts, prostheses are not limbs; they are synthetic versions of natural things. Pain, too, is natural. By analogy, painmaker pain feels just like the real thing, but it is not natural, so it is not pain. It is artificial pain, which means there may yet be a single physical, *neural* type onto which pain maps. The possibility of artificial mental states, in natural minds or otherwise, does not rule out the natural identity of mind and brain. Alternatively, if such artifice would, in fact, constitute the genuine article, then the silicon state would count as a bona fide brain state and would then be susceptible to the strategies recommended above.

So far, I have argued that one-to-many mental mapping is not as obvious as it is often taken to be. But suppose it is, the above proposals notwithstanding. Does this imply that mental properties are not physical? It is often taken to mean this. This move, however, relies on a disanalogy between mental and physical types that is less clearcut than it seems. Mental types are unlike physical types, it is held, because the latter either are, or smoothly reduce to, fundamental properties. While, for heat, we have the equation [temperature = mean kinetic energy], there probably or principally can be no equation [pain = x] where the x is non-disjunctive. Temperature is a physical property because it enters into physical laws, and it enters into physical laws because it is univocally realized by—and therefore type identical to—mean kinetic energy. But pain is multiply realizable by—and therefore at best token identical to—physical states. So although pain enters into psychological laws, and although it is realized by genuine physical types, it is not itself a genuine physical type.

My defense of type identity will be indirect. Taking temperature and pain as paradigm cases, I argue against the putative disanalogy between mental and physical properties. The first thing worth pointing out is that not all physical properties are non-disjunctive. Epidermal properties are realized by an indefinite disjunction of epitheleal types, and these are physical in no weaker sense than neural properties, which tend to be glossed as straightforwardly physical. Of course epithelea fall within the domain of biology, which is a special science, where multiple realization is precisely what token identity expects. But one gets the sense that such things are assimilated all too easily into an imposing, amorphous "physics" for the purpose of mandating a stark and misleading mental/physical dichotomy. A better example is solidity, which is not only physical but multiply realizable. The claim that solidity is not a strictly physical type is not plausible.

Mark Wilson raises an even better example—[temperature = mean kinetic energy]—the very paradigm case so often used to contrast physical with mental properties.[5] This equation is strictly true for ideal gases but only approximately true for real gases—this by itself is not much of a problem. What is a problem, though, is that the equation is true only within a very narrow domain. It does not tell us what temperature is in all substances, some of the exceptions being vacuums and solids at low temperature. It may seem, then, that temperature is multiply realizable only in the nominal sense that strictly physical types include not temperature-as-such but rather temperature-of-a-solid, temperature-of-a-gas, and so on. The disanalogy is thus apparently preservable by allowing for a finer-grained typology for heat, where [temperature = mean kinetic energy] is understood to define temperature-of-a-gas. But this, as I argued earlier, is precisely the sort of consideration that would motivate us to adopt a finer-grained typology for pain. Besides which, there is an entire sub-discipline of physics—thermodynamics—that takes temperature as a genuine physical type irrespective of what kind of substance has it. Indeed, in thermodynamics, temperature-as-such is a necessary coordinate for describing a physical system. There are other reasons to reject the disanalogy. First, the molecules of a gas can have different properties (locations, velocities, constituent atoms) and still realize the same temperature. Worse, [temperature = mean kinetic energy] does not even tell us what temperature is in all gases, for the mean kinetic energy of the constituent molecules of a dense gas at low temperature depends on density *and* temperature. Temperature is a disjunctive type even if we limit ourselves to talking about the temperature of gases. Ironically, this undercuts the paradigm case of physical properties taken to contrast with mental types. We have to admit that almost nothing, including many physical properties, is *strictly* physical, or else abandon the notion that disjunctive types cannot be physical types in the strictest sense.

This presents a dilemma. Either qualia are type identical to physical states (in that we allow disjunctive types to be strictly physical types), or we have token identity *all the way*, including most of physics. We have to give up the disanalogy, one way or the other. But either way, we avoid problems about the mental being peculiar or too weakly anchored to the physical world. Yet the whole motivation for saying that things like qualia are not strictly physical types is that things like temperature strictly are. Although I think type identity is the preferable option, the advocate of token identity can bite the bullet and say that physics is a special science no less special than the rest. However, no one thinks that temperature is not a genuine physical type, even if it is disjunctive, and so the rationale for denying qualia the same status is no longer clear. If temperature is a genuine physical type, then there is no reason why pain cannot be as well. I want to emphasize again that I have been arguing against the disanalogy often taken to favor token identity (and functionalism, for that matter) over type identity, rather than arguing directly that a type can be *strictly* identified with the disjunction of its realizers. What I have not said much about is whether identities of this sort are ultimately allowable. This is a key question, and I will leave it open, except to reiterate that we can deny type identity only on pain of having to deny that temperature is a physical property. However, whether we can deny this is another matter, for a physics without temperature, solidity, and the like, seems too far removed from the discipline as we know it. The point is, type identity can be preserved, and if it cannot, no matter. Mental states are physical. So are mental properties.

L ET US SUPPOSE that we are all good naturalists and take for granted that consciousness is part of the physical world. Mental states and properties are neural or, at least, broadly speaking, physical. Is this a solution to the mind/body problem? Does it solve, more specifically, the problem of consciousness? The answer depends on what kind of naturalist you are. If you take the problem to be one of articulating the relationship between mind and brain, then, yes, that is done. What remains is to go into the lab and find out what it is about the brain that generates consciousness, what its neural correlates are. In its most extreme form, this is what might be called "easy naturalism," the view that there is no problem of consciousness, for qualia are just features of the brain, pure and simple.[1] Such extreme naturalism ignores the fact that consciousness appears to be metaphysically peculiar. It cannot seem to fit in the physical world. Without some argument against the anomalousness of consciousness, the extreme naturalist seems to be missing the point, or worse, trying to cheat. I have argued at some length that consciousness is not metaphysically peculiar, at least not in the ways it is often taken to be. But there seems to be something more to the problem, something deep and difficult, so difficult, in fact, that it is almost insurmountable. The relationship between consciousness and the brain poses a unique *conceptual* problem which threatens to undermine all the good metaphysical work we have done. It threatens at the very least to show that such a picture is woefully incomplete. I will argue in this chapter that, while there is a conceptual gap between consciousness and its neural correlates, neither are the consequences of this terribly important, nor is the gap as difficult to close as it is often taken to be.

What exactly is this gap? David Chalmers explains it this way: consciousness "arises from a physical basis, but we have no good explanation of *why* or *how* it so arises. Why should physical processing give rise to such a rich inner life at all?"[2] (emphasis added). In other words, why and how do the neural correlates of consciousness give rise to consciousness? This is a hard problem. In fact, it is *the* hard problem. When we investigate consciousness in the lab, we learn a lot about subjects' abilities to discriminate and otherwise deal with stimuli; about how the brain integrates and transmits information and how internal states are accessed and reported by subjects; and about the limits of attention, the scope of deliberate behaviour, and many other things besides. But these are easy problems. Whatever we learn about the brain and the processes it implements, no such knowledge will give us even a toehold on explaining why and how consciousness arises. Such scientific knowledge as we are able to gather does not touch the hard problem, which always reappears in vibrant full force no matter what the lab reports say. Another way to put the problem is to say that there is an explanatory gap between consciousness and any account of its physical basis.[3] Any such account will fail to explain how and why the physical determinants determine what they do. But surely it would be relevant to our understanding of consciousness that its neural correlates are, say, oscillations in the 40-hz range. Not really, says Chalmers, for discovering the neural correlates is one of the easy problems. It has to be done in the lab, and if it is done in the lab, it is easy. Such discovery would not tell us why it is 40-hz oscillations, rather than oscillations in some other range, or some other correlates altogether, that are accompanied by experience. Nor would it tell us why experience accompanies those correlates. Why the company is required, and how it is invited in, would remain the mysteries they are.

As Chalmers sees it, the hard problem is so very hard that we cannot solve it without radical metaphysical rejigging. We have to undertake an extensive overhaul of our fundamental view of the universe. This may seem a little extreme, but this is not the half of it. Chalmers recommends that we abandon the materialist view of the universe that serves science so well, until, that is, it abuts on the hard problem. But if we discard matter from the metaphysical fundament, with what should we replace it? Not mind, surely. This would evaporate the problem rather than recasting it. Chalmers's candidate is *information*. He proposes an "it-from-bit" metaphysics, which includes mind and matter in the furniture of the universe—these are the "its"—although the substance underlying them, the ultimate stuff of the universe, is neither mental nor material but informational.[4] I admire Chalmers for broaching such metaphysical speculations and for finding a motivation for them. Philosophers used to do this sort of thing all the time. Almost no one does it any more, though, because, for better or worse, it is viewed as an indulgence. If solving the hard problem requires this sort of indulgence, that would seem to many to be a reductio of the hard problem. It is one thing to say that the substance underlying mind and matter is information, but it is quite unclear how we are supposed to gets the "its" from the "bits." On the one hand, the proposal is a kind of neutral monism, where mind and matter are "logically constructed" out of some neutral substance, in this case information. Bertrand Russell once proposed a variety of neutral monism, one which posited sense data as the ultimate neutral stuff. But where the data of sensation seem more mental than neutral, information seems more material, or objective at least, in which case the hard problem reemerges vis-à-vis the informational correlates of consciousness, with no net gain. On the other hand, Chalmers's proposal is a variety of dual aspect theory, where mind and matter are simply different aspects of the same metaphysical fundament. What ground do we thereby gain on the hard problem? Why and how do the neural correlates of consciousness give rise to consciousness? The answer is, *they do not*; they are different aspects of information. But then, again, we have a different hard problem, that of why and how information comes to have its phenomenal aspect. Chalmers cannot say it just does, because such an answer will not suffice for the hard problem in its original formulation. Worse, if information has a phenomenal aspect, and the universe is made of information, this means consciousness is *everywhere*. Even if Chalmers solves the hard problem peculiar to his own radical worldview, his panpsychism is anything but faithful to the spirit of the original hard problem and constitutes, again, a good reductio of it. If solving the hard problem means going *this* far, we have likely made a mistake in our original diagnosis. It would be best to stick, for now, with a less radical metaphysics.

What other considerations might help soften the hard problem? Consider Chalmers's formulation of it, which is a two-part question: *why* do the correlates generate consciousness, and *how* do they do so? Notice that Chalmers does not ask why or how the *brain* generates consciousness, for these presumably admit of more or less easy answers. We can answer the question of how the brain generates consciousness by citing the neural correlates. If the 40-hz hypothesis is true, then the brain generates consciousness, simply enough, by firing at 40-hz. We can also answer the question of why the brain generates consciousness by telling the right story about the biological purpose it serves, or simply by citing the role it plays in our mental and neural economy. But Chalmers's question is about the correlates themselves, not about the brain in general, which means that any description of what the correlates are or what they do will not address the question. Yet, while it makes sense to ask why and how the brain generates consciousness, it is not clear whether it makes sense to ask why and how the correlates do. The why question admits of easy answers, or else is nonsense, or else comes down to the question of why there is consciousness at all. Consider some analogous questions. Why are there spirochetes at all? Why is there something rather than nothing? The how question, too, seems to admit of easy answers. If materialism is, as I have argued, true, then the correlates do not give rise to, but rather are, consciousness. It gives rise to itself by being what it is. Presumably what is lurking in the how question is the epiphenomenalist suspicion. But we have quelled that. If anything, the hard how question is yet another strike against epiphenomenalism. Consider whether it is sensible to ask why, or how, H_2O gives rise to water.[5] That water is H_2O is supposed to provide a straightforward explanation of why water has the observable properties it does, why it is wet, transparent, colourless, tasteless, why it freezes at 0° and boils at 100°, everything. But if it is true that consciousness is 40-hz oscillations, this supposedly does not straightforwardly explain why experiences feel the way they do, or why there should be such things as experiences. This, again, is the kind of unwarranted disanalogy that pops up time after time in the philosophy of mind. As we have already seen, the mental is not metaphysically peculiar in the sort of way such disanalogies require. The hard gap seems particularly salient, but only because of a corresponding gap in our knowledge. When we discover the neural correlates of consciousness, and they are ramified as such in the scientific canon, this will inform our concept of consciousness no less than the equation of water and H_2O. Kripke cannot have it both ways, and Chalmers cannot either.

Perhaps the gap between consciousness and the brain cannot be fully closed until we know for sure what the neural correlates are and what makes them so special. There are various hypotheses afoot, but we do not have a clear enough picture as yet. This may sound reasonable, but it is a bit premature. Even without knowing what the correlates are, we can still work toward closing the hard gap. To see how we might get some closure, I want to revisit a view of the problem that illustrates the tension between hard and easy naturalism. Despite the pessimism this view suggests, a pessimism every bit the equal of the full hard gap, it also suggests, in spite of itself, an illuminating and, I think, fruitful way of framing the problem. The view is Thomas Nagel's.[6] As he says, facts about a subject's consciousness are facts about what it is like to be that subject, what it is like for you to be you, what it is like for me to be me. An inherently subjective point of view, my consciousness is my perspective on myself and the world around me. The character of one's subjective point of view, in this sense, depends on what kind of creature one is and on every internal and external nuance of the phenomenal here-and-now, shaped as these are by the present and past, mental procedures learned and innate, and so much more. But this is not the only point of view one can have. Science yields an objective point of view, abstracted beyond the confines of singular subjectivities. It can tell us much about those objectively accessible processes that give rise to consciousness, but it seems impossible that we could ever have an objective theory of something intrinsically viewed from within. If such a theory could be constructed, we would be able to know what it is like to have a consciousness other than our own. We would be able to know what it is like to be a bat, for instance, what it is like to echolocate, to participate in a bat's form of life, to behave in a batly fashion. But this, it seems, is something we could never know. The mechanics of echolocative perception is one thing. But we cannot imagine what it is like to be an echolocative perceiver, what it is like to be a bat, which means that we cannot have the sort of understanding required by an objective theory of consciousness in the relevant sense. Perhaps one day we may be able to construct such a theory, in, as Nagel says, "the distant intellectual future," but not yet by a long shot. We cannot imagine what such a theory would be like, much less the kind of understanding that it is supposed to give us.

Nagel's is arguably the twentieth century's definitive statement of the problem of consciousness. Much as the problem seems hopeless as he articulates it, Nagel has his critics, and one among them who deserves special mention is Kathleen Akins.[7] She provides the perfect counterpoint to Nagel, engaging his version of the hard problem directly from the vantage of a hard-line, lab-friendly naturalist position. When you study bats, she says, and review the scientific literature on them, you discover that bats are not so utterly alien and hard to understand as Nagel makes them seem. Bat behaviour is pretty simple, it is easily predictable, and it is more or less hardwired. Their insect-hunting and -catching patterns, for instance, are both relatively few and readily analyzable. There is no big mystery about what bats do and how they do it. Bat brains are likewise structurally and functionally simple, as one might expect. We know a lot about how echolocative perception works, and we build machines—radar and, better, sonar—that allow us to access information in the same kind of way that bats do, albeit indirectly, and for different purposes, naturally. But what is it like for the bat? Well, Akins says, that is the thing. Assuming, as is plausible, that a substantial degree of cortical sophistication is necessary for consciousness, and given that bat behaviour and bat brains are such simple things, it is not obvious, in the first place, that there *is* anything it is like to be a bat. The behavioural and cortical sophistication are not there. Bats brains cannot manage it. Besides, to the extent we may have to admit that bats are conscious, we know a lot about what it is like to be one, all there is to know, in fact. If there is something it is like, it is like having a kind of radar display that levers one into simple behaviour patterns of flying, searching, insect-catching, and so on. The more we know about the mechanisms involved, the less analogical and more complete our understanding, in the limit of which nothing of bat consciousness is omitted.

The tension between hard and easy naturalism could not be more beautifully illustrated than in the Nagel/Akins debate. Nagel privileges the first-person perspective, and deems it irreducible to an objective point of view in any terms. The prospect is not even, for now at least, an intelligible one. Akins, on the other hand, privileges the third-person perspective, in terms of which all bona fide facts about anything, in particular bat consciousness, are knowable as such. The two seem quite clearly to be talking past each other. Nagel might be seen to ignore the fact that empirical investigation can enrich our understanding of other people's and other creatures' consciousness, not to mention our own. By the same token, Akins might be seen to mistake what Nagel intends the bat example to do. For instance, if bats turn out to be insentient, they can be replaced in the example by other creatures that echolocate and are clearly sentient, such as dolphins. When parties talk past each other like this, it is often wise to approach the matter in a mediating vein: maybe the problem lies in privileging either the first- or the third-person perspective over the other. Assume that Nagel is right to insist that we cannot imagine, in sufficiently rich detail, what it is like to be a bat. Assume, again, that Akins is right to insist that all bona fide facts concerning what it is like to be a bat are, at least in principle, knowable by us. Is there any way to avoid the apparent contradiction? I think there is. Recall the example of Mary, the utopian neuroscientist. As I argued earlier, Mary knows what it is like to see red even before her inaugural colour quale. She cannot imagine what it will be like, but she knows what it is like without being able to imagine it, because her complete physical knowledge gives her the capacity to recognize her inaugural quale. By analogy, if we had complete physical knowledge of bats, we might not be able to imagine what it is like to echolocate as a bat does, but we would have the same kind of recognitional wherewithal that Mary does. If this seems unlikely, the reason it does is probably twofold. First, complete physical knowledge might well be beyond our ken. Second, natural law seems to rule out the possibility that we could have the sort of inaugural bat quale analogous to Mary's inaugural colour quale. People walk out of rooms all the time. They never turn into bats. That does not matter, though, because if such knowledge *were* within our ken, then we would also know, in the relevant sense, what it is like to be a bat.

Suppose that we cannot avail ourselves of this mediating tack, and, despite the doubts we have raised as to its legitimacy, the hard problem resurfaces. Is there any way to close the gap without broaching the radical sort of metaphysical rejigging that Chalmers proposes and that we are right to resist? I think there is. There are three kinds of things in the universe, falling into concentric classes. There are physical objects, some of which are living, and some of the living things are conscious.[8] What is the ultimate nature of matter, of life, of consciousness? These are the great mysteries. Maybe taking the hard gap seriously obligates us to tackle corresponding hard problems in physics and biology, and this may constitute yet another reductio of the hard problem. How do microphysical properties give rise to macrophysical properties, and how do physicochemical properties give rise to a living being? That is not my concern. Taking the hard gap seriously, now, I am going to try to close it. Despite Nagel's claim that we have no clue, as yet, as to what kind of theory would make the relationship between consciousness and the brain intelligible, he does suggest where we might start looking for one. The very subjective point of view that causes all the trouble is, ironically, the source of a useful gap-bridging concept. The *desideratum*, I suggest, is not a functional description of consciousness, but rather a concept sufficiently close to the heart of consciousness to capture its essential features, yet elastic enough to be used not only in a description of consciousness, but in descriptions both of inanimate objects and of living things. Nagel's unwitting candidate is *perspective*. It is a plausible candidate, because consciousness is essentially perspectival, and both inanimate objects and living beings can be understood in perspectival terms. Working with the concept of perspective will allow us to recast the hard gap in such a way that it appears somewhat easier to bridge than it does on Chalmers's original formulation. Together with other mediating concepts, this will also allow us to do bridgework, not in one giant leap, which seems inordinate if not impossible, but in successive small steps.

Material objects are, and are essentially, extended in space. Their occupation of points in space defines their shape. But points in space are points of perspective on other points in space. Objects appear one way or another, depending on the vantage point from which they are seen. They present different, incomplete "views" of themselves to different points in space. Living things, though, do not just occupy perspective, as inanimate objects do. They are no less susceptible to physical forces, but, where inanimate objects are passive to the forces which affect them, living things respond to environmental stimuli, which abut on the perspective they occupy. The scope of affective stimuli and the kinds of response effected are reflected and, in the case of insentient life, determined by the kind of creature in question. Because such responses are in service of biological imperatives, an insentient creature may be said to *exhibit*, through its responses, a perspective on the stimuli to which they are informationally sensitive, the success of which matters in terms of the organism's biological fitness. A conscious being, though, does not only occupy and exhibit perspective, it also *has* perspective on itself and the world around it. Other perspectives are broadcast far and wide, while had perspectives are "slimcast" each to a subject. What distinguishes the slimcast is that it does not only matter to the organism in a biological sense, it also has meaning, or a kind of meaning-potential, *for* the organism *as* a subject. Indeed, an insentient being is not a subject in the same robust sense that a sentient being is. The hard gap, then, is that between had and merely exhibited perspectives. Blindsight patients occupy perspective on the stimuli they discriminate, and, as they are informationally sensitive to such stimuli, they also exhibit perspective. The crucial thing they lack is the kind of perspective which constitutes consciousness. They do not *have* one. The stimuli have no meaning for them as subjects, as though someone else is doing the job of reliable discrimination. "Someone" else is, of course, the system. As a physical object, the brain *occupies* perspective, and as the body's informational headquarters, it also *exhibits* perspective. But while, in normal vision, it also gives a subsequently had perspective to the subject, in blindsight, it does not. What does the brain do to turn the exhibited perspective of blindsight into the had perspective of normal vision? To say that a being is conscious is to say that there is something it is like to be that being. This means that the subject has a perspective on itself and the world around it. The elements of this perspective are distinct from those of a merely exhibited perspective, as they have a kind of meaning, or meaning-potential, for the subject. How does an internal state, which would otherwise be unconscious, come to possess such meaning? It presumably enters into a distinctive kind of process, perhaps a self-scanning process. The idea that the brain scans itself is not difficult to fathom, nor is the idea of brain states possessing meaning. So why, and how, do the correlates give rise to consciousness? To become the correlates proper, they enter into a kind of process, plausibly self-scanning, which gives them a kind of meaning, or meaning-potential, making them elements of a perspective, the very kind of perspective to which consciousness reduces. Thus do we achieve, step by step, a bridge across the gap.

Solutions to the hard problem, such as the one I have offered, cannot help but be a bit speculative. Do not forget Chalmers's call to metaphysical revolt. My solution has at least the relative advantage of measures less draconian. But, as with Chalmers's solution, mine falls short of completeness. If Chalmers must answer the question of why and how the informational correlates of consciousness give rise to consciousness, I, too, must answer the question of why and how 40-hz oscillations, or self-scanning, or wide availability, or activity in some special neural structure endows the sort of meaning that makes for a had perspective. Incidentally, maybe all these hypotheses are right. Maybe consciousness is realized by 40-hz oscillations peculiar to certain structures, is achieved via self-scanning, and yields wide availability. That would be nice. Of course, one can always pull up hard questions in true Chalmers style, however narrow the gaps in however complete a picture of the matter we have. But such questions have to come to an end somewhere. As consciousness is not metaphysically peculiar in the first place, we should not be too bothered about the conceptual conundrum of the hard gap. Perhaps eagerly anticipated further discoveries about consciousness will close the gap completely or at least fill in the details in some such solution as the one I have offered. We need more information from the lab. Supposing otherwise is an armchair presumption.

BERTRAND RUSSELL ONCE SAID that philosophy is a matter of starting off with something so obvious that no one would bother to say it, and ending with something so outlandish, so bizarre, that no one would believe it. What I have done so far is to invert this process. We began with blindsight, a phenomenon so bizarre that, but for the hard data we have on it, no one would believe it. And we have taken it, step by step, to a theory of mind that has been something of an establishment view since the demise of logical behaviourism, as well as appealing, on certain intuitions, to common sense. I do not mean to suggest that most people are materialists. They are not. Most people are dualists of one stripe or another. Common sense is not as common as its name implies. Our examination of blindsight and consciousness is not over yet, however. There are other areas of philosophical concern on which blindsight is likely to bear. Some of these topics, the more significant ones, I think, have not yet been tapped by philosophers. Other, less significant topics have been tapped, but minimally, and they deserve, despite their relative unimportance, further scrutiny. The more important topics are the theory of knowledge and the conceptual foundations of vision science, because the way blindsight bears on them has interesting implications for the role consciousness plays in knowledge generally and visual perception in particular. I will explore the philosophical application of blindsight to the theory of knowledge in this chapter and its application to the conceptual foundations of vision science in the next. But first I will discuss those minimally tapped topics I mentioned, one of which pertains, indirectly, to the theory of knowledge.

One topic is colour theory, on which blindsight bears as a locus of intuition haggling, at least, for the simple reason that, in the absence of visual experience, patients can and do perceive colour. The most intuitive interpretation of this for colour theory seems to be that colours are genuine physical properties.[1] For various reasons, we might want to hold that colours are, like so many other properties it seems, disjunctive physical types. For instance, we cannot identify colours with properties like surface reflectance, for there are colours "by emission," as with flame and neon lights, as well as colours by reflectance. Plus, the existence of metamers—as when red and yellow make orange—make it seem that we have a disjunctive type even in the case of surface reflectance. However, just as there are strategies to employ getting rid of one-to-many mental mapping, we can adopt similar strategies in getting rid of one-to-many colour mapping. We might generalize across the disjuncts, and type identify colours with some property like average wavelength within a certain range, just as, on a more naive view of temperature, we identify temperature with mean kinetic energy. If we cannot, that does not matter. Just as one-to-many mapping does not rule out the physicality of temperature, so too would such mapping fail to rule out the physicality of colour. Of course, it is open to those who think that colours are subjective—that they are properties not of physical objects but of experiences themselves—to say that what blindsight patients perceive are not colours themselves, but rather the physical properties that tend, in the right conditions, to cause them.[2] This is rather strikingly similar to the epiphenomenalist's position that the qualia blindsight patients lack are mere products of the brain states in virtue of which normal perceivers have them. Similar, yes, and subject, then, to similar kinds of criticism. We may not *have* to fit colours into the physical world, but if we can—and we can—and since it is desirable, why not?

Another debate concerns whether blindsight patients have perceptual beliefs about the stimuli they discriminate. When, for instance, a patient "guesses" that a stimulus is X- rather than O-shaped, do they *believe* that it is X-shaped? This may not seem to be a very interesting question. Indeed, most philosophers who mention it treat it in a very cursory fashion. But if it can be shown that blindsight patients do have perceptual beliefs about the contents of their blind fields, then blindsight will be readily applicable to the theory of knowledge in interesting ways. Despite the potential fruits of such application, however, philosophers have not exploited it. I am inclined to think that patients do have such beliefs, in part because we can make a good *prima facie* case for it and in part because the arguments against it are rather anemic. In the *prima facie* case, patients discriminate many stimulus properties, quite clearly evincing such perceptual judgments as "The stimulus is red," "The stimulus is X-shaped," and so on. For this to be so, a patient must have certain internal (brain) states that *mean* "The stimulus is red," "The stimulus is X-shaped," and so on. Perceptual judgments have content, and perceptual beliefs are the most natural, non-phenomenal, content-bearing things to infer that patients have. In fact, ascribing perceptual beliefs to patients is part of the best explanation of how blindsight works, psychologically speaking. One objection to this view is that, since patients think they are guessing, since they do not *believe* they have perceptual beliefs, much less reliable ones, they do not.[3] Of course, if patients have such beliefs, it is pretty clear that such beliefs are unconscious. Patients may be aware of what they are inclined to "guess," but they are not aware of these inclinations as expressions of belief. This coheres with what we know of patients' epistemic situation. They believe, falsely, that they lack information about the stimuli, and they believe, falsely, that they cannot deploy such information, and so it is natural to expect that they would also believe, falsely, that they lack perceptual beliefs.

So the hypothesis is that patients have unconscious beliefs. How is it that such an internal state remains unconscious? We become aware of internal states by introspection. It may be that if blindsight patients have perceptual beliefs, the reason they remain unconscious is that the introspective mechanisms systematically fail. But patients' lack of awareness cannot be pinned on the failure of introspective mechanisms, for these mechanisms in blindsight remain intact. The damage is to the primary visual cortex, while the introspective mechanisms are further up the line, as it were. As patients' introspective mechanisms are not to blame, this suggests that, as far as perceptual beliefs go, there is nothing there to introspect.[4] This objection is subtler than the first. In response, let me say, first, that it is not clear that introspective mechanisms are unscathed in blindsight. It is plausible that they are, but the more important point is that a system may fail, and fail systematically, despite being perfectly operative. A perfectly operative system may "fail" through no fault of its own if, for instance, it lacks the necessary input. Were it to get such input, it would perform as it should, but since it does not get the input, it does not perform. The necessary input may include the state to be introspected, but it may also include other things. The qualia patients lack are plausibly necessary for the higher-order processing of which patients are incapable, as well as for the ability to access and deploy information spontaneously. In the same way, a retriever who is very good at fetching sticks may fail to retrieve one when the necessary cue, such as the sweep of the throwing arm, is missing. Although introspective mechanisms may not be to blame, this does not mean there is nothing to introspect.

It seems that for an internal state to count as a perceptual belief, it has to have a certain degree of cognitive sophistication or informational richness. But, in comparison with normal perceivers, blindsight patients' performance, however astounding it may be, is rather rudimentary. While they can, admittedly, perceive relationships between blind and intact field stimuli, they cannot perceive relationships between stimuli which lie in the blind field. In short, it seems that blindsight does not involve the cognitive sophistication and informational richness that perceptual beliefs require and so, it seems, cannot involve perceptual beliefs. While most objections to blindsight belief are given in somewhat too cursory a fashion, this objection, by Gerald Vision, is articulated and elaborated at some length.[5] While I will not respond directly to all of Vision's points—there are many of them—I think his objections can be countered with some very general remarks. First, why could more basic content not enter into perceptual beliefs? Ordinary perceptual beliefs run a wide range of complexity from "Those are Picassos" to "That's a chair" to "That's red." It is hardly clear that an internal state which bears the content "The stimulus is red" or "The stimulus is X-shaped" lacks the sort of cognitive sophistication that would disqualify it as a perceptual belief. If I, as a normal perceiver, were asked to discriminate the colour of a stimulus, and I came out with the judgment "The stimulus is red," surely that would express an authentic perceptual belief. How is it, then, that the internal state of a patient who makes the *same* judgment as I do does not have a similarly authentic perceptual belief? But even if Vision is right about such basic cases, the blind-field-in-relation-to-intact-field cases cannot be so easily dismissed. If you place a word across a patient's visual field such that he sees the ambiguous NK on the right, and you ask him to "guess" whether the word is BANK or TANK, his disambiguation will be reliable. If *that* is not cognitively sophisticated, it is certainly sophisticated enough.

Even so, it might be that patients' internal states, content-bearing and sophisticated as they may be, fall short of being authentic perceptual beliefs. They might be what philosophers call *subdoxastic states*— "pieces" of belief, or belief-like states that are missing some key ingredient. If we could find the "belief box" in the brain, where belief content and only belief content is inscribed, then we could determine whether blindsight patients have perceptual beliefs by finding out whether blind field content pops up in the belief box. I admit that there may be no such thing as blindsight belief, only subdoxastic blindsight states, but I do not think so. Consider what is by now the unexceptional fact that blindsight is an aberrant visual phenomenon involving deficiencies of consciousness and perceptual function, admittedly much less a deficiency of function than we would expect. To account for this phenomenon, we have to deny that patients have some of the things enjoyed by normal perceivers, such as visual qualia and spontaneous function. My question is whether we have to deny patients perceptual beliefs as well. This matters, for when we account for aberrant phenomena of this sort, we should only deny what we have to in distinguishing the aberrant case from the normal one. When water beads on smooth surfaces, for instance, we explain this by citing the fact that friction is non-negligible on most normal surfaces, where water does not bead, while in the aberrant case, where water does bead, it is negligible. We do not have to cite some other deficiency. In fact, unless we have to do so either as a consequence of explanation or on independent grounds, we cannot. Call this *the principle of parsimonious denial*. We do not have to deny that blindsight patients have perceptual beliefs, either in accounting for the phenomenon or as a consequence of such an account. The only independent reason we may have for the denial is the idea that perceptual beliefs depend, as they typically seem to, on perceptual experience. But this is precisely the kind of intuition to which blindsight runs counter. In the rest of this chapter, then, I will assume that patients have authentic perceptual beliefs.

As a first step in applying blindsight to the theory of knowledge, consider Moore's paradox.[6] Imagine that someone says, "The cat is on the mat, but I do not believe it." Such statements have the form "P, but I do not believe that P," but they are not self-contradictory, although they certainly seem to be. From a normal perceiver, who sees the cat on the mat, such a statement would sound odd, because to assert that P is usually taken to express the belief that P, the very belief that is denied in the second part of the statement. Notice that this type of utterance is more or less exactly what we expect from a blindsight patient. There is no apparent contradiction in the blindsight case, however, because when a patient says, "The stimulus is X-shaped," this judgment, while reliable and although expressive of a belief, is not a proper assertion, much less warranted as such. The patient is not *claiming* that the stimulus is X-shaped, they are "guessing." They lack access to evidence that favours their judgment. As such, blindsight is strikingly similar to a thought-experiment which exemplifes the central debate in epistemology. The case is that of Mr. Truetemp.[7] Mr. Truetemp has a "tempucomp" surgically implanted in his brain. Not only does this tempucomp reliably tell temperature, it informs Truetemp's thoughts, causing him to have beliefs about what the temperature is. Not knowing that the tempucomp has been implanted, he is in a situation similar to that of the blindsight patient who is unaware that she has blindsight. Here is the key question. When Truetemp judges that it is, say, 20.5°, does he *know* it is 20.5°? In the same way, when a blindsight patient judges that a stimulus is X-shaped, does she *know* it is X-shaped?

Philosophers have traditionally analyzed knowledge into three components. To know that P is, first, to believe that P; second, for P to be true; and third, to be justified in believing that P.[8] Epistemology is primarily concerned with justification, and there are, broadly speaking, two schools of thoughts on the matter. *Externalists* see justification as a matter of reliability, or something similar, while *internalists* see it as a matter of warrant. Unlike mere reliability, warrant requires that the subject have, and have reflective access to, sufficiently good reasons to assert what they believe. Since both the blindsight patient and Mr. Truetemp have reliably generated true beliefs, the question of whether they have knowledge depends on whether they have justification, which in turn depends on whether justification is a matter of reliability or warrant. Everyone would agree, I think, that when the blindsight patient and Mr. Truetemp become aware of their respective conditions—the patient knows she has blindsight, Truetemp knows about the tempucomp—their beliefs do constitute knowledge. The question is whether they have knowledge *before* they find this out. If they do not, then internalism is true. If they do, then externalism is true. So which is it? Either way, the implications of blindsight will be telling.

Let us assume that, for justification, we need to have reflective access to warrant-conferring reasons. Despite the reliability of their beliefs, since patients do not have reflective access to warrant-conferring reasons, they lack justification, hence knowledge. The missing ingredient is awareness of the fact that they have blindsight: when they come to know that they are blindsighted, they know that their judgments are reliable, and, so, they have warrant for asserting what they believe. On subsequent trials, they will know that the X-shaped stimuli are X-shaped, since their judgments to this effect are warrantedly assertible. Given this, we should expect that self-avowed blindsighters would not "guess" anymore. Warranted assertibility will yield warranted assertion. That is the internalist's story, and it sounds plausible enough, from a certain perspective. The interesting thing about the internalist story is that internalism does not follow from it. Notice that part of the story is predictive. Patients whose judgments are warrantedly assertible will warrantedly assert those judgments. Reflective access to warrant-conferring reasons is supposed to yield warranted assertions. For the patient to have such access, the reasons must be *evident*, and evident reasons, to be evident, must *move* the subject accordingly. The interesting thing is that, in the case of many self-avowed blindsighters, they are *not* so moved. They keep on "guessing." They lack confidence, despite the good inductive grounds they have to exhibit such confidence. This means that even if warrant is necessary for justification, it is not by itself sufficient. Or, if it is sufficient, knowledge has another ingredient besides justified true belief. This extra ingredient is a certain degree of certainty.[9] It is supposed to come with warrant, it seems like it should, but it does not, so it is extra.

All of this, however, is on the assumption that warrant is indeed necessary for knowledge, but this is far from obvious. One reason is that the appeal to tacit knowledge, which, by definition, subjects do not have reflective access to, is an indispensable part of psychological explanation.[10] Whether it is knowledge of deep grammar, the mechanics of tying a shoelace, or blindsight belief, we are going to run up against the need, somewhere along the line, to posit tacit knowledge. Indeed, the reflective access requirement seems to rule many species, which are not only sentient but more obviously sapient, out of the class of knowers. The self-unavowed blindsighter knows that the X-shaped stimulus is X-shaped, but they do not know that they know. If you think knowing requires knowing that you know, consider the infinite regress of having, then, to know that you know that you know, and to know that you know that you know that you know, and so on. It should not, after all, be surprising that externalism gives a better account of blindsight, for perception, and the varieties thereof, are where externalist theories really shine.[11] Blindsight, as a case of perceptual knowledge, provides very good support for externalism, as well it seems it should. But the justification debate does not turn solely on perception. Self-unavowed patients may, it seems, have justified beliefs and sufficiently justified beliefs at that. But by the same token, the self-avowed blindsighter has yet *more* justification than her ignorant counterpart. Warranted assertibility enlarges justification. This is especially clear where, as in normal cases, it moves us to have confidence in our judgments. It is not reliability that we are after in day-to-day epistemic life. In scientific practice, we arguably do not even care about reliability. We care about hypotheses giving us reliable predictions, of course, but the formulation, confirmation, modification, and rejection of such hypotheses are all done on a warranted assertibility basis, having access to, being moved by, and giving reasons for assertions. If blindsight beliefs are justified, then their justification seems radically unlike the sort of justification we are after in, say, the sciences. You cannot do science, or even engage in day-to-day argument with minimal competence, except on the basis of such justification as warrant provides. The kicker is that, despite valiant and extensive attempts to explain warrant in terms of reliability, the prospects for such reduction are dim, which leaves us, once again, with the same old debate.

In resolving this debate, there are several strategies we might employ, not all of them equally viable. We might insist on one of the two accounts and defend it to the last in light of whatever counterexamples are furnished by the world or imagination. But that would be too easy. More ambitiously, we might try and hybridize the two. This would mean that justification requires both reliability *and* warrant. However, while this strategy is a good one, often overlooked in areas of philosophical concern where it can potentially work, it does not seem a viable one for resolving this debate. While warrant may augment the justification of perceptual beliefs, it seems an excessive stricture to require. Likewise, it seems excessive to require reliability where warrant is all we have to go on. If one day scientific method is superceded by *schmience*, or if, less drastically, some of our present theories turn out to be false, that does not mean we are unjustified in believing them now. How could it? A false theory may yield reliable predictions, of course, but it will also give us a systematically unreliable picture of the world. Yet, if all the evidence we now have points to such a theory, how could we not be justified now in believing it? Since hybridization seems not to work, we should acknowledge that blindsight patients have knowledge in one sense and lack it in another. They have reliable but unassertible true beliefs. What they have is tacit knowledge. What they lack is explicit knowledge. It might be said that, in blindsight, the *system* knows while the *subject* does not. But that is a somewhat loose way to put it. We resolve the debate, in any case, not by endorsing one account over the other, or by hybridizing both, but by shunting each to its own domain. This is a species of *contextualism*, according to which what is required for justification is variable, depending on the context.[12] While some versions of contextualism emphasize variations in social norms, epistemic interests, values, and the like, and have been justly criticized on that basis, this contextualism is different. It emphasizes differences only in terms of the subject matter to which beliefs pertain and the means by which such beliefs are acquired. Beliefs about electrons require warrant, but beliefs about the shape of an X-shaped stimulus do not. Perceptual beliefs, as well as those arising involuntarily from other mental faculties, such as memory, are amenable to reliabilist justification. Warrant may enlarge justification here, but it is not necessary. In the theoretical reaches of science and other areas where reliability cannot be judged, warrant is not only necessary, it is sufficient. In between these domains lies the vast stock of most day-to-day beliefs, for which, perhaps, both kinds of justification are needed. The picture of justification that emerges here is one of overlapping kinds, and while this is not a grand unified theory of knowledge, it is plausible. It is sensitive to the data, at least, and that has to count for something. Things are not always as simple as we would like them to be.

This view of justification indicates, as we should hope, that consciousness plays a special epistemic role in our mental economy. In fact, it is precisely this consideration that leads Nick Humphrey to consider blindsight a sort of "pure" perceptual knowledge, pure in that the lack of visual experience precludes patients' awareness of their knowledge as knowledge or as *theirs*.[13] For this reason, patients do not feel justified in acting as inclined, nor can they recognize their inclinations as anything more than guesses, made under duress at that. In particular, they cannot feel warranted in asserting what they "guess." If that is pure perceptual knowledge, uninfected, as it were, by subject-involvement, then in the normal case, experience facilitates a perceiver's recognition of their perceptual knowledge, both as knowledge and as theirs. Normal perceivers thus feel justified and confident in acting as inclined. Their inclinations, unlike those of blindsight patients, are rationalized for them. They feel warranted in asserting their perceptual beliefs and are so warranted, because the warrant-conferring reasons are available to them in consciousness. Warrant *depends* on consciousness. A perceptual belief can be warranted, in part, by the experience which gives rise to it, for the experience contains information from which the belief is extracted. But beliefs can also be warranted by cohering with other beliefs. If consciousness is the means by which information becomes widely available in the brain, then this aspect of warrant is also dependent on consciousness. Unconscious beliefs may cohere with the rest of the subject's belief system, but they will not be *actively* coherent in a warrant-relevant way. It is in the augmentation of basic justification that consciousness plays a part. It increases the justification of reliably justified beliefs and opens the door to investigation in areas where reliability is not a factor, where warrant is all we have to go on. Consciousness is the *sine qua non* of investigation as such.

IN THIS, the last philosophical application of blindsight to be discussed in this book, we turn to several difficult and interesting issues in perception theory, from the viability of certain models of the visual system to the conceptual foundations of vision science. That blindsight should bear on such issues is not surprising. The phenomenon is a striking counterexample to the idea that visual function depends on visual consciousness. It shows that behaviourally effective visual function does not depend on visual consciousness either and that an intentional, *contentful* response to a stimulus need not depend on consciousness of the stimulus. More than this, it even shows, as I have argued, and paradoxical as it may seem, that perceptual beliefs in the visual domain can likewise be had without any concomitant experience. With such implications lurking at the back of one's mind, one would not think blindsight possible. But the data change all that. While these implications are significant, however, what I focus on in this chapter is the idea of perceptual *inference*. An inference, roughly speaking, is reasoning, moving, as it were, from premises to conclusions. You can conclude, for instance, "Socrates is mortal" from the premises "All men are mortal" and "Socrates is a man." Inferential theories of perception take perception, or at least most cases of it, to involve moving from "premises"—the bare, minimal data provided by the world—to a "conclusion"—the perception itself. Blindsight has been adduced, and I think rightly, in support of inferential theories of perception. It has also been discussed in connection with a certain "two-streams" model of the visual system, one which, perhaps ironically, may allow resolution of one of the most important debates in perception theory today, that between inferential and direct theories of perception. This will in turn suggest something rather surprising about the functional role of consciousness.

Let us consider how blindsight supports inferential theories of perception. First, the more sophisticated a perception is, the more likely it is that it is an inference, regardless of whether it is the subject or the system that is doing the inferring. For example, some paintings are Picassos, and so there is such a property as *being a Picasso*. Some objects have it; most do not. It is permissible to speak of perceiving such properties. Some people can look at a painting like *Guernica* and tell that it is a Picasso. Such perceptions, if we can call them that, clearly involve inferences. The point, though, is this. If we can show that a kind of perception involves inferences, then the more basic the perception is, the greater the scope of perceptual inference and the stronger the evidence it provides for inferential theories. Blindsight is a *very* basic kind of perception. It is near the other end of the spectrum from the perception of Picasso-ness. As such, if we can show that blindsight is inferential, then this is very strong evidence in favour of inferential theories. Can we show this? I think so. Patients only perform well when forced to choose between a pair of provided options. They only judge that a stimulus is, say, X-shaped when given some such choice as X- *or* O-shaped. This looks remarkably like a disjunctive syllogism, which has the form: X or O, not O, therefore X. The provided options make for a first, disjunctive premise, while the patient's judgment is the conclusion. The missing premise, in this case, is "not O," as though the visual information the system provides is somehow a kind of *negative information*. Perhaps, though, the system simply has the information that the stimulus is X-shaped, but cannot deploy such information until it shows up in the disjunction. I think we could test for this by giving patients more options to choose from, say, A- or X- or O- or N-shaped. If blindsight works by disjunctive syllogism, a series of such syllogisms would have to be performed, and this would require greater response time, as well as being more tightly bound to memory than simply hitting on the right disjunct once the experimenter gives it. Even if patients do not unconsciously perform a disjunctive syllogism, however, the suggestion of an inference of some sort or other is in no way diminished.

Inferential theories take a "bottom-up" view of perceptual processes. The senses receive a very minimal amount of information directly from the world. These simple representations are built up into more and more complex representations until, finally, these processes issue in what we would recognize as the perception of an object. Specialized subsystems, or modules, receive input from more basic subsystems, and, by performing the special inferences or *computations* for which they are designed, they generate output for use in further processing. For the most part, on this view, the traffic is one-way. The higher-level stuff is produced by, rather than having much effect on, the lower-level stuff. In particular, visual representations and processes are largely unaffected by cognitive states like beliefs and desires. Vision is, in this sense, cognitively impenetrable. To encapsulate the bottom-up view in a slogan, what you see is not affected by what you believe. Nor, for that matter, is what you see affected by what you want. This may seem obvious, but there is a rival view which takes a "top-down" view of perceptual processes. On this view, the higher-order stuff can significantly affect the lower-level stuff. This may seem a bit strange, especially in the extreme. You cannot generate any visual representation you want. Whatever the merits of the top-down view, and however much such things as feedback loops make some strain of the top-down view seem, in a sense, plausible, there is plenty of good evidence against it, and blindsight constitutes part of it.[1] The perceptual processes underlying blindsight do not seem to exhibit top-down effects. If they did, then the fact that patients *believe* they do not possess, much less that they can deploy, visual information, should significantly affect blindsight performance, if not outright nullify it. But in terms of performance, there is little difference between patients who do not know they have blindsight and those who know they do. This huge cognitive difference has little to no effect on patients' performance, and, if any cognitive difference is to have such an effect, this is it. Indeed, the very fact that blindsight exists seriously undermines the claim to any substantial top-down effects in visual processing. By thus undermining a rival of the bottom-up view, blindsight supports inferential theories of perception.

Another rival to inferential theories is the view that perception is, in some sense, direct. Now some perception has to be direct insofar as perceptual inference does not arise *ex nihilo*. It cannot. However minimal the data perceptual systems pick up from the world directly, an inference has to rely on such data as "premises." Without premises, there is no inference. The direct/inferential perception debate is not about, and in no way turns on, whether there is any direct pick-up from the world. It is not about *whether*, it is about *how much*. It is about scope, in other words. But we must be careful to distinguish different versions of the direct/inferential distinction. In the more traditional sense, a perception is direct if the property in question is immediately available, to the perceiver, in perceptual consciousness. It is inferential if it has to be inferred, perhaps tacitly, from the perceptual qualia. For instance, shape may be immediately available to consciousness—one can have a shape quale—while distance may have to be inferred from such cues as the position of the object, its apparent size, the type of object it is, and so on. The interesting thing here is that blindsight, as a kind of perception, is neither direct nor inferential in this sense of the distinction. An importantly different sense of the direct/inferential distinction is as follows. One may be immediately aware, in the traditional sense, of an object's apparent shape, but this perception may not be direct—and it probably is not—insofar as the visual system, to yield that quale at all, must perform a number of inferences on the data it receives at the retina. The 3-D representation of an object, available to consciousness and mentally rotatable in imagination, is built up out of simpler representations of edges, contours, contrasts, textures, and so on.[2] The perception is indirect in that the system must perform inferences to get it and direct inasmuch as the system picks up the basic information non-inferentially. The direct view of perception, in its most extreme form, has it that *all* perceivable properties, including 3-D shape, distance, and all apparently inferred properties, are "affordances" picked up non-inferentially.[3] Blindsight is telling here, for it seems to involve unconscious inference, even in such basic tasks as judging the 2-D shape of stimuli. If 2-D perception is inferential, then 3-D perception has to be.

We will come back to this in a minute. The route will be roundabout but appropriate, and in the course of taking it, we will look at another discussion of blindsight in connection with perception theory. Early on, you may remember, we looked at the question of how, from a neuroscientific point of view, blindsight works. V1 is damaged in blindsight, cutting off the main visual pathway from the retina to the rest of the brain, effectively precluding conscious vision in the corresponding part of the visual field. Another significant pathway is, however, left intact, and it is hypothesized that this intact pathway is what underwrites blindsight. This other pathway bypasses V1, naturally, and terminates in the posterior parietal lobe at the upper back of the brain, above and slightly forward of V1. In normal perceivers, the main visual pathway splits at V1 into two distinct, dissociable streams, one which terminates, as does the blindsight pathway, in the posterior parietal lobe. This is the dorsal stream. The other—the ventral stream—runs to other cortical centres, visual and otherwise. It is hypothesized, by David Milner and Mel Goodale, that the ventral stream subserves the cognitive integration of visual information, while the dorsal stream subserves visually guided action.[4] The two streams do not communicate with each other, much less, dissociable as they are, do they depend on each other. This makes for an interesting but potentially problematic account of blindsight. Since the blindsight stream leaves off where the dorsal stream does, then blindsight must be, at root, a kind of visually guided action, with slight if any cognitive integration. In cued action tasks, reaching for objects, catching balls, this seems to be the case. But this does not seem to be the case in forced-choice discrimination tasks. It seems there has to be cognitive integration, not just motor deployment, of visual information. The apparently inferential character of such discriminations and the not insignificant sophistication of some of them make it clear. The answer, I suggest, is to admit that while the dorsal and ventral streams are dissociable and, thus, independent in that sense, they nonetheless are able to communicate with each other. The information has to get through somehow. In a way, this hypothesis is a natural one. To have systems that are dissociable, yet able to inform and check up on each other, is an evolutionary advantage.

The two-streams model of vision provides a potential means of resolving the direct/inferential perception debate. It should be noted that the debate emerges, in part, from different views of what the purpose of perception is. Is it for acquiring knowledge of one's environment, as it seems to be? Inferential theories emphasize the acquisition and processing of information, while direct theories de-emphasize these in favor of more basic biological purposes. What is important is not inferring things about the world, it is responding on cue. While the purpose of perception, on the inferential view, is knowledge acquisition, on the direct view, it is adaptive motor response, pure and simple. But although perception obviously serves biological purposes, it also serves, surely, the purpose of knowledge acquisition. This is so, if for no other reason, because the capacity for deliberative action is itself a pretty adaptive thing to have. Goodale, this time with Keith Humphrey, proposes that the debate can be resolved on the two-streams model of vision.[5] Perception simply has *both* purposes. The ventral stream is devoted to knowledge aquisition, while the dorsal stream is geared for visually guided action. This interpretation of the two-streams model thus harmonizes the erstwhile opposite approaches of direct and inferential theories *vis-à-vis* the purpose of perception. However, it seems less a resolution of the fundamental schism, and more the modest concession to the direct view that *some* visual processes are geared for action, independent of such knowledge as may otherwise result. This does not, by itself, imply that any such processes are direct. If they are inferential, then whether they are geared for action or not, they do not encroach at all on the territory of the inferential view.

I like to think that more can be done to resolve the direct/inferential perception debate. The Goodale/Humphrey proposal is a provocative one as is, but I will try to take it one step further. This will, of necessity, be more than a little bit speculative. Let us suppose that the dorsal stream is not only geared for immediate action but also, strictly speaking, direct perception. If so, then the fundamental schism between direct and inferential views will be resolved, because perception will be, in an important sense, both inferential *and* direct. If neither stream has exclusive rights to visual input, and, while one stream processes it inferentially, in the other it leads directly to action, then this would be such a fundamental resolution. Why might one suppose that the debate lends itself, even assuming the two-streams model, to such a resolution? The answer is another question: what is the point of having an action-geared system that bypasses cognitive integration? Knowledge acquisition is adaptive, after all, but it is not *always* adaptive. Knowledge acquisition takes time, and some situations require very quick responses, the quicker the better, in fact, quicker than waiting for inferences to be performed first. Sometimes the system needs to react directly on cue, *before* cognition and consciousness have a chance to enter the fray. The need for such direct responses is plausible. Sometimes cognition and consciousness catch up after the fact. Let me illustrate. I used to play softball, and in my teens I became quite a good infielder. When I was in top form, I was good, as infielders have to be, at catching "bad hops," where a well-hit grounder hits a stone or imperfection and suddenly veers off at an unexpected angle. Several times I protected my face from what surely would have been serious injury. The biological purpose of such abilities is obvious. What I noticed was this. When I fielded especially fast bad hops, my body seemed to react *before I did*. My gloved hand would move, almost of its own accord, to where, in order to catch the ball, it had to be. It was a ballistic response, immediate and skillful, and it would always surprise me. Indeed, such ballistic response is what usually clued me in to the fact that there was a bad hop at all. I would feel it in reaction, then see it in success, like a quick-time equivalent of blindsight or visual agnosia. On the two-streams model, what allowed me to do this was the dorsal stream, and I think it is plausible that, when such response time is absolutely crucial, and word from cognition and consciousness arrives too late, the perceptual processes are, in fact, direct. Something—call it an "action vector"—moves my hand before I do, before I can. In a sense, then, it might be said that perception is both inferential and direct. But, of course, this must be qualified. We must bridle speculation to a comfortable trot. Dorsal stream processes may be inferential after all, but, even so, they are interpretable rightly, in a non-trivial way, as *implementing* direct perception. Also, more importantly, even if my speculation is true, many perceivables, probably most, are not amenable, it seems, to non-inferential perception. There certainly are no Picasso "affordances" out there. My speculation, then, poses little threat to establishment views in vision science. It is mere speculation, at that.

At the beginning of this, the last chapter in this rather short book, I promised that my discussion would suggest something odd, something surprising, about the functional role of consciousness. One thing I noticed about fielding bad hops was that, however much skill I had, the more I focused on trying to *see* where the ball was going, the less able I was to exhibit that skill. I was discernibly slower, for instance, and often too late, not to mention imprecise in my movements. Too intently pursued, then, consciousness seems to inhibit more immediate responses. That is the surprise I promised. An otherwise good thing can hinder on occasion. What worked for me—and I mean this in a non-loaded way—was, if you will, a willing suspension of consciousness. While, in itself, this remark is not terribly insightful, it does suggest, if nothing else, that of all things, studies of physical activity may provide further deep insights into the nature of consciousness in particular and the mind in general. With that, and in hopes of discoveries to come, we draw this chapter and this book to a close.

NOTES

INTRODUCTION

1 This is a loaded way of putting it, as there is some controversy over whether blindsight patients lack visual experience or have some kind of *unconscious* visual experience. No doubt the phenomenon is a sort of unconscious vision, involving sensory representations of which the subject is unaware. But, as I argue later in the book, it is not only unnecessary but conceptually infelicitous to speak of such representations as experiences, albeit quite peculiar ones. For introductory purposes, my loaded description should suffice.

2 The earliest philosophical commentary I know of is Mellor (1977). The case-study is Weiskrantz (1986).

3 I worked on Holt (1998) under the guidance of William Demopoulos, Ausonio Marras, and Keith Humphrey, to all of whom I owe a deep debt of gratitude. Thanks also, as always, to Larry Holt.

4 Tye (1995), pp. 19-21. Actually, it is *super* blindsight—a thought experiment based on the phenomenon itself—that makes Tye's top ten list. The phenomenon is seen, then, less as a problem and more as the basis for a problem for theories of consciousness.

5 Ryle (1949), pp. 17-18.

6 Armstrong (1970), pp. 70-72. See also Armstrong (1968).

7 See, for instance, Putnam (1960), Fodor (1974), and Lewis (1980).

8 See, for instance, Block (1980).

9 I borrow this helpful way of carving up the philosophical space from Flanagan (1992), pp. 1-2. I am, like Flanagan, a constructive naturalist, one who believes it is possible to have a scientifically respectable—and informed—theory of consciousness. Later, I will discuss three different kinds of constructive naturalism, which view the problem of consciousness as a pseudo-problem, a hard problem, and a moderate one, respectively. Moderates see it as a conceptual problem, not metaphysical, rather than both, or neither.

CHAPTER 1

1 Pöppel *et al.* (1973), Weiskrantz *et al.* (1974), and Sanders *et al.* (1974).

2 Riddoch (1917), Holmes (1918).

3 Klüver (1936), (1941), and (1942). Psychophysicists often speak of colour perception as necessarily involving, or even consisting in, colour experience. See, for instance, Stoerig (1998). Nonetheless, it does not seem untoward to say that blindsight patients discriminate colours. Nothing important in this book hinges on my terminological preference.

4 Humphrey (1970) and (1974). See also Humphrey (1992), pp. 88-93, as well as Stoerig & Cowey (1997), pp. 551-552.

5 Details given here are from Weiskrantz (1986), pp. 140-74 and (1997), pp. 16-70, Cowey & Stoerig (1991), Marcel (1983) and (1998), and correspondence with Marcel cited in Carruthers (1989), p. 260.

6 See Barbur et al. (1993) and Weiskrantz (1997), pp. 143-45.

7 See Fendrich et al. (1992) and Gazzaniga et al. (1994) vs. Weiskrantz (1995) and (1997), pp. 152-53.

8 See especially Campion et al. (1983) and replies in Werth (1983) and Weiskrantz (1986), pp. 146-52. See also criticisms attributed to Zeki and replied to in Weiskrantz (1997), pp. 245-51.

9 The non-definability critique is made in Campion et al. (1983) and replied to in Werth (1983), where several definitions are listed. See also Weiskrantz's definition (1986), p. 166. On the question of blindsight in normal perceivers, see Kolb & Braun (1995). Methodological concerns are raised in Graves & Jones (1992), and Reingold & Merikle (1993).

10 Carruthers (1989), pp. 259-60.

11 See, as discussed, Crick & Koch (1990) and Baars (1988).

CHAPTER 2

1 Among them, Natsoulas (1982), p. 106 and (1997), pp. 27-28; Carruthers (1989), p. 260; Nelkin (1994), p. 543 and (1996), pp. 177-179. Happy to admit the possibility are Churchland (1980), pp. 192-193, and Chalmers (1995), pp. 200-201 and (1996), p. 227. Of Chalmers in particular this is surprising. Weiskrantz (1986), p. 166 defines blindsight as "visual capacity in a field defect in the absence of acknowledged awareness" and so may seem to be broaching the same conceptual infelicity. He is not, however. Rather, he is using "awareness" in a more technical sense which neither is synonymous with, nor implies, consciousness per se.

2 Jacket blurb on Weiskrantz (1997).

3 Flanagan (1992), pp. 55-56.

4 Accounts of blind touch are presented in Paillard et al. (1983) and Rossetti et al. (1995). A brief account of deaf hearing is presented in Michel & Peronnet (1980). While "numbsense" was coined for residual touch in the absence of tactual consciousness, I think "numbtouch" would be better, reserving "numbsense" for the superordinate category, including blindsight, numbtouch, and deaf hearing.

5 For achromatopsia, see Heywood *et al.* (1991). LM is described in Zihl *et al.* (1983). See Weiskrantz (1997), p. 31 for a description of LM's abilities, communicated by Peter McLeod, some of whose findings appear in McLeod *et al.* (1996).

6 Marshall & Halligan (1988).

7 Milner & Goodale (1995).

8 For studies of prosopagnosia, see Bauer (1984) and Tranel & Damasio (1985). For a nice account of HM's implicit memory, see Flanagan (1992), pp. 16-19.

9 See especially Sperry (1974). For speculation inspired by split-brain cases, see Nagel (1971); Puccetti (1973); Parfit (1984), pp. 245-48; and Penrose (1989), pp. 496-99.

10 On metacontrast, see Dennett & Kinsbourne (1992). For good critical commentary thereon, and for a nice account of the Broadbent filtering effect, see Flanagan (1992), pp. 81-84, and pp. 13-15, respectively.

CHAPTER 3

1 Churchland (1983), p. 82. The same point is put with sometimes less, sometimes greater stridency in Churchland (1980), pp. 192-193; Churchland (1984), p. 143; Churchland (1986), pp. 228; and Churchland (1988), p. 288.

2 Churchland (1984), pp. 45-46. The eliminativist gambit, as I discuss it here, is presented quite succinctly in Churchland (1984), pp. 43-49. See also Churchland (1986), pp. 310-12.

3 Flanagan (1992), pp. 23, 33, and Horst (1995) make similar points, although Flanagan seems to overestimate the explanatory role or consciousness, while Horst perhaps underestimates it.

4 Non-reductive materialism is explicated clearly in Marras (1993) and (1994).

5 For a thorough critique of the Churchlands on reduction, see Endicott (1998). Churchland's more recent view (1985) is that the mental is eliminable no matter how smooth or rough the reduction, which effectively rules out the mind *a priori*!

6 See Penfield (1958) for an account of his famous experiments correlating neuro-stimulation and phenomenal experience.

7 See Crick & Koch (1990). 40-hz phase-locked oscillations are hypothesized to be the neural correlates of consciousness because they seem to have the right sort of temporal and information-binding properties. This illustrates the point that mental and neural types are specified on a mutually informative basis.

CHAPTER 4

1 Dennett (1991), p. 328. Dennett is really a master of the rhetorical turn of phrase, of which this is by no means the best example.

2 See Stoerig & Cowey (1997), p. 549. See also Humphrey (1970), (1974), and (1992), pp. 88-89, where he reminisces, with discernible tenderness, about working with Helen. See Chapter 1.

3 Dennett (1991), p. 332. Despite the insistence by Dennett that blindsight really is a rudimentary sort of vision, it is interesting to note that this claim supports a view to which Dennett himself is opposed—computationalism. If blindsight is low-level vision, this confirms the basic tenet of the computational paradigm that much mental processing is *not available to consciousness*. It is to William Demopoulos that I owe this point.

4 The imagined patient is so characterized by Block (1994), p. 215. But it is not clear what the point of this characterization is, as Block is hardly a devout epiphenomenalist. Super and normal blindsighters alike are neurologically different from us. Zombies also lack qualia, but they are not neurologically different from us. Unlike blindsighters, zombies are not obviously imaginable and, indeed, are ruled out by materialism. In both cases, we have the independence of some visual function from visual experience. But the analogy ends there.

5 For other criticisms of Dennett on blindsight, see McCauley (1993) and Weiskrantz (1997), pp. 60, 63, 70, 178. McCauley objects that Dennett's attack on qualia through blindsight is inconsistent with the recent empirical findings presented in Ramachandran & Gregory (1991) and moreover begs the question against the realist. Weiskrantz points out minor errors—too minor to mention here—in Dennett's account of certain blindsight experiments and is rightly uncertain as to how they impugn, rather than support, realism about qualia. Perhaps understandably, Weiskrantz takes super blindsight more as a serious research proposal than as a thought-experiment designed to undermine the realist position.

6 Block (1994), p. 215 takes it to show a difference between access consciousness, which the imagined patient and normal perceivers have, and phenomenal consciousness, which the former lacks. I will criticize this distinction later on. Tye (1995), pp. 19-21, claims that the difference between normal vision and super blindsight is precisely the sort of thing we should expect a theory of consciousness to articulate. It seems a good theory should also make sense of the difference between vision and normal blindsight. See Siewert (1998), pp. 76-84, for interesting variations on the super blindsight theme that stress the significance of consciousness.

7 Dennett (1988). For the intuition-pumps discussed below, see pp. 73 and 61; 52, 60, 62; 50, 57, 63; and 49-50, respectively. Dennett has since claimed to have relaxed his stand against qualia and the mental generally. Advertisements notwithstanding, it is not clear that Dennett can relax his stand without *really* admitting the existence of qualia.

8 Dennett (1988), p. 60, admits that to set this up at all we would have to quantify over neural states and processes responsible for "qualia," but he insists that these could not be qualia. Why not? For "the simple reason that one's epistemic relation to them is *exactly* the same as one's epistemic relation to such external, but readily—if fallibly—detectable properties as room temperature and weight" (emphasis in original). But temperature and weight have to be *inferred*, in a very robust sense, unlike qualia. Furthermore, we infer such things *from* our qualia, whether precisely with the aid of thermometers and scales, or loosely by mere phenomenal feel. Qualia are our first line of inference, our last line of defense. See Flanagan (1992), p. 77.

CHAPTER 5

1 McGinn (1997), p. 86. Many of the points to follow appear in Holt (1999).

2 Searle (1983), p. 47. Those who doubt the existence of visual experience did subsequently look at blindsight, but found it more grist for their mills than most realists did, including Searle. For variations on Searle's point, see Siewert (1998), pp. 73-84.

3 Cam (1985), p. 361. The particular view targeted by Cam is that proposed in Dennett (1969). Even if phenomenal awareness is awareness purely of one's speech dispositions, Cam argues, *that* awareness must have a raw feel to it to count as awareness at all. Dennett, I think, does not want to render phenomenal awareness as awareness of speech dispositions, but rather awareness *tout court* as dispositions *simpliciter*. Oddly enough, Cam does not mention that a "phenomenology" based on *speech* dispositions is implausible simply because there are, surely, sentient species incapable of language.

4 Hysterics would be distinguishable from blindsighters in that the former could be cured by appropriate therapy. This is not possible with blindsight, as patients really are cortically blind. Other sorts of cure are, however, possible, at least in principle. We cannot yet repair damaged V1, but one day maybe we will.

5 Flanagan (1992), pp. 114-15.

6 Shallice (1988), pp. 307, 316.

7 Fodor (1968), pp. 7-8.

8 Fodor (1968), pp. 5-6.

CHAPTER 6

1 Flanagan (1992), pp. 141-42.

2 Dretske (1995), p. 122. Dretske's take on blindsight might seem to be in conflict with his general account of the relationship between sensory representations (qualia) and conceptual representations (intentional states), namely, that the latter depend on the former as the analog source of the information they digitize. See Dretske (1981), Chs. 5-6. But in blindsight, as Dretske admits, we have unconscious intentional states generated without qualia. The natural way out is to admit that not all sensory representations are conscious. Indeed, blindsight aside, phenomena like subliminal perception make it clear that some sensory representations have to be unconscious all the way along. It is clear even without such phenomena, as qualia themselves depend on (unconscious) low-level sensory representations.

3 Velmans (1991). Those who have attributed similar arguments to some of their colleagues include Dennett (1991), p. 325; Tye (1993), p. 20; and Chalmers (1996), p. 253. A philosopher who comes close to doing so is McGinn (1991), pp. 110-19. However, McGinn thinks that blindsight illustrates how qualia are causally idle—that they have only a minimal causal role. McGinn's mistake is to drastically overestimate what blindsight patients can do. For other objections to Velmans, see Block (1991) and Dretske (1991).

4 See Block (1995). An earlier version of this argument is cited in Flanagan (1992), pp. 145-47.

5 Chalmers (1996), p. 227. The notion that the description of blindsight is underdetermined is possibly shared by Churchland (1980), pp. 192-193, and Vision (1997), pp. 126-127. Chalmers has gained notoriety of late by pressing the "hard" problem of consciousness, which is to answer the question of why and how the neural correlates of qualia "give rise" to qualia. See Chalmers (1995), p. 201 and (1996), p. 4. I grant that the *how* question seems hard, but it is harder to see the motivation for the *why*. The crux really seems to be "Why is there consciousness at all?" which is comparable to "Why are there spirochetes at all?" or more aptly "Why is there something rather than nothing?"

6 Weiskrantz (1986), pp. 167-68 and Weiskrantz *et al.* (1995). This is an interesting phenomenon. It seems as though phenomenal residua somehow interfere with peak performance, which is the opposite of what one would expect, and supports the notion that blindsight really is a different form of vision and not a degraded form of normal vision.

7 I am assuming here, as epiphenomenalists do, that the physical world is causally closed and that the mental is metaphysically dependent on the physical. If qualia are non-physical, then they are epiphenomenal. Jackson might be interpreted as prescinding from the usual assumptions and arguing for the weaker claim that qualia are simply non-physical and that epiphenomenalism is at least possible. But often enough he is taken to be arguing for the stronger, more interesting conclusion. The thought-experiment originates in Jackson (1982) and is further developed in Jackson (1986). For discussion see Horgan (1984) and Tye (1989), pp. 133-50.

8 See in particular Russell (1910-1911), although the distinction emerges earlier in Russell's work. Tacit knowledge, of which blindsight is an example *par excellence*, seems anathema to the view that knowledge either is or decomposes into knowledge by acquaintance. However, the dependence is apparently still viable in the case of *explicit* knowledge.

9 See Feigl (1967), pp. 64-71. It is sometimes said that Western philosophy consists in footnotes to Plato. Philosophy of mind since the 1950s, in certain important respects, consists in footnotes to Feigl. Note that Tye (1989), p. 139, makes mention of Russell but omits mention of Feigl. Raymont (1995), pp. 723-24, dismisses Feigl as a mere predecessor of Tye's.

10 Brian Loar argues that phenomenal concepts are *recognitional* concepts, so it seems he would endorse this kind of approach to the Mary case. But he also argues that mere recognition is insufficient for having a phenomenal concept, as we can recognize things in a blindsight-like way without being able to imagine the relevant experiences. See Loar (1990), pp. 97-98. However, blindsight "recognition" is not recognition at all, but discrimination. While I agree that not just any *discriminative* ability will suffice for a phenomenal concept, it is far less clear that a recognitional ability will not suffice. Nothing really hangs on this, though, as the concept/property distinction requires that even if Mary fails to know what it is like to see red (in the sense of having the phenomenal concept), this does not rule out that phenomenal properties are physical properties.

CHAPTER 7

1 Kripke (1972), pp. 150-52. I think that this objection to materialism can be rejected without engaging directly either Kripke's semantics or his take on the distinction between necessary and contingent truth. The same goes for many similarly inspired arguments, of which Kripke's is conveniently representative as a paradigm case.

2 The classic versions of this argument are, of course, found in Putnam (1960), Fodor (1974), and Lewis (1980).

3 See Flanagan (1992), pp. 6, 56-57, and 145-47.

4 Philosophers are a curious bunch when it comes to the possibility of artificial minds, inflaming them unduly from their usual reserve. Many seem to accept the following tempting but false dichotomy. (1) Computers cannot do what we can, and since having a mind requires doing what we can do, artificial minds are impossible. (2) Computers can do what we can, and since they do not have minds, *we do not either*, or at least much of what we think about the mind is false. But (1) seems chauvinistic, and (2) seems extreme. Despite this, both views are championed in the philosophy of mind. But there is a way out.

Can computers do what we can? Yes. Are artificial minds possible? Yes. That is the way out.

5 Wilson (1985), p. 228.

CHAPTER 8

1 A good example of such "easy naturalism" is Searle (1984), pp. 13-27.
2 Chalmers (1995), p. 201. See also the much more extensive Chalmers (1996).
3 Levine (1983).
4 Chalmers (1995), pp. 215-17.
5 This line is pushed in Hardcastle (1996), pp. 10-11.
6 Nagel (1974) and (1986), pp. 13-66.
7 Akins (1993).
8 I do not mean to suggest that artificial minds are impossible. Perhaps some non-living things could be conscious. Perhaps, though, one must be alive to be conscious. Insofar as artificial minds are *artificial*, they may inhere in equally artificial life.

CHAPTER 9

1 Nelkin (1994), p. 543, seems to draw this implication, although this reading might be more charitable than true. What is clear is that he takes patients to have an unconscious kind of qualia, which is surprising given the conclusion he apparently draws. This puts him in cahoots with Block and others whose similar views were criticized earlier. See also Nelkin (1996).
2 This interpretation is suggested, but not proposed, by Landesman (1993).
3 Vision (1997), p. 126. This is corrected in Vision (1998), p. 154. The view that patients have unconscious beliefs is separately proposed in Mellor (1977) and Heil (1983), p. 80.
4 Tye (1993), p. 30.
5 Vision (1998).
6 Moore (1942), p. 542.
7 Lehrer (1993), pp. 312-13.
8 *Modulo* Gettier (1963). Gettier argues, famously, that justified true belief—an analysis of knowledge inherited from Plato himself—is not in fact sufficient for knowledge. Here is one example. Bob and I apply for a job, and I have it on good authority that he will get it. He shows me that he has 10 coins in his pocket, and so I believe that the person who is going to get the job has 10 coins in his pocket. As it turns out, however, I get the job, and, unbeknownst to me, I have 10 coins in my pocket. I have a justified true belief that the person who will be hired has 10 coins, but I do not, it seems, have knowl-

edge of this. The problem seems to be that I infer my belief from a false premise, to wit, that Bob will get the job. We may think, then, that knowledge is justified true belief that is *not* derived from false beliefs. The no-false-beliefs condition does not seem to work however. See Pojman (1993), pp. 131-32. Say I have good reason to think that, in a student election, candidate A will get all the residence vote (30 per cent), all the off-campus vote (30 per cent), and the fraternity vote (30 per cent). I infer, then, that A will win. Suppose I am right about the other two blocks, but wrong about the residence vote. I know, it seems, that A will win, even though my belief is based, in part, on a false belief. So the no-false-beliefs condition will not work. What will? I suggest this. Replace the no-false-beliefs condition with a sufficient-true-beliefs condition. A justified true belief will be knowledge so long as there are sufficient true beliefs in the inference-base to warrant, on their own, the inference in question. The Gettier case fails this condition, while the election case passes, both verdicts according, as they should, with intuition.

9   This is suggested in Malcolm (1952).

10 Fodor (1981).

11 Perhaps the most important contemporary epistemologist, a vanguard of externalism, is Alvin I. Goldman. See Goldman (1967) and (1979) for statements of his early causal, and later reliabilist, accounts of justification. Blindsight might seem a counterexample to the view of perceptual knowledge proposed in Goldman (1976), in which he argues that a perceptual belief, to count as knowledge, must be caused by the fact that makes it true *in the absence of relevant alternatives*. If I see a barn, and believe it is a barn, I will not know it is a barn if there are look-alike false barn façades about. In a blindsight trial, when, say, a patient judges that a stimulus is X-shaped rather than O-shaped, the possibility of its being O-shaped seems a relevant alternative. But it is not. Relevant alternatives have to fool the system such that the system would make the same judgment in either case. But the patient would judge that the stimulus is O-shaped if it were O-shaped. The possibility of the stimulus being O-shaped is a look-alike alternative, but not a relevant alternative. So no counterexample here.

12 See, for instance, Annis (1978).

13 Humphrey (1992), p. 92. See also Marcel (1988).

CHAPTER 10

1   See Pylyshyn (1999), and Vaina (1995).

2   The classic account is, of course, Marr (1982), especially pp. 8-38.

3   See, for instance, Gibson (1979).

4   Milner & Goodale (1995), pp. 67-86.

5   Goodale & Humphrey (1998).

Akins, K. (1993). What Is It Like to Be Boring and Myopic? In B. Dahlbom (ed.). *Dennett and His Critics*. Oxford: Blackwell. 124-60.

Annis, D. (1978). A Contextual Theory of Epistemic Justification. *American Philosophical Quarterly 15*, 213-19.

Armstrong, D.M. (1968). *A Materialist Theory of Mind*. London: Routledge & Kegan Paul.

Armstrong, D.M. (1970). The Nature of Mind. In C.V. Borst (ed.). *The Mind/Brain Identity Theory*. London: Macmillan. 67-79.

Baars, B. (1988). *A Cognitive Theory of Consciousness*. Cambridge: Cambridge University Press.

Barbur, J.L., Watson, J.D.G., Franckowiak, R.S.J., & Zeki, S. (1993). Conscious Visual Perception Without V1. *Brain 116*, 1293-302.

Bauer, R.M. (1984). Autonomic Recognition of Names and Faces in Prosopagnosia: A Neuropsychological Application of the Guilty Knowledge Test. *Neuropsychologia 22*, 457-69.

Block, N. (1980). Troubles with Functionalism. In N. Block (ed.). *Readings in Philosophy of Psychology*. 2 vols. Cambridge, MA: Harvard University Press. 268-305.

Block, N. (1991). Evidence Against Epiphenomenalism. *Behavioral and Brain Sciences 14*, 670-72.

Block, N. (1994). Consciousness. In S. Guttenplan (ed.). *A Companion to the Philosophy of Mind*. Oxford: Blackwell. 210-19.

Block, N. (1995). On a Confusion about a Function of Consciousness. *Behavioral and Brain Sciences 18*, 227-47.

Cam, P. (1985). Phenomenology and Speech Dispositions. *Philosophical Studies 47*, 357-68.

Campion, J., Latto, R., & Smith, Y.M. (1983). Is Blindsight an Effect of Scattered Light, Spared Cortex, and Near-Threshold Vision? *Behavioral and Brain Sciences 6*, 423-28.

Carruthers, P. (1989). Brute Experience. *Journal of Philosophy 86*, 258-69.

Chalmers, D.J. (1995). Facing up to the Problem of Consciousness. *Journal of Consciousness Studies 2*, 200-19.

Chalmers, D.J. (1996). *The Conscious Mind: In Search of a Fundamental Theory*. New York: Oxford University Press.

Churchland, P.M. (1984). *Matter and Consciousness*. Cambridge, MA: The MIT Press.

Churchland, P.M. (1985). Reduction, Qualia, and the Direct Introspection of Brain States. *Journal of Philosophy 82*, 8-28.

Churchland, P.S. (1980). A Perspective on Mind-Brain Research. *Journal of Philosophy 77*, 185-207.

Churchland, P.S. (1983). Consciousness: The Transmutation of a Concept. *Pacific Philosophical Quarterly 64*, 80-95.

Churchland, P.S. (1986). *Neurophilosophy: Toward a Unified Science of the Mind/Brain*. Cambridge, MA: The MIT Press.

Churchland, P.S. (1988). Reduction and the Neurobiological Basis of Consciousness. In Marcel & Bisiach, 273-304.

Cowey A., & Stoerig, P. (1991). The Neurobiology of Blindsight. *Trends in Neurosciences 14*, 140-45.

Crick, F.H., & Koch, C. (1990). Towards a Neurobiological Theory of Consciousness. *Seminars in the Neurosciences 2*, 263-75.

Dennett, D.C. (1969). *Content and Consciousness*. London: Routledge & Kegan Paul.

Dennett, D.C. (1988). Quining Qualia. In Marcel & Bisiach, 42-77.

Dennett, D.C. (1991). *Consciousness Explained*. New York: Little, Brown & Co.

Dennett, D.C., & Kinsbourne, M. (1992). Time and the Observer: The Where and When of Consciousness. *Behavioral and Brain Sciences 15*, 183-247.

Dretske, F. (1981). *Knowledge and the Flow of Information*. Cambridge, MA: The MIT Press.

Dretske, F. (1991). Conscious Acts and Their Objects. *Behavioral and Brain Sciences 14*, 676-77.

Dretske, F. (1995). *Naturalizing the Mind*. Cambridge, MA: The MIT Press.

Endicott, R.P. (1998). Collapse of the New Wave. *Journal of Philosophy 95*, 53-72.

Feigl, H. (1958). The "Mental" and the "Physical." In H. Feigl, M. Scriven, & G. Maxwell (eds.). *Minnesota Studies in the Philosophy of Science 2*, 370-497. Reprinted (1967) *The "Mental" and the "Physical."* Minneapolis: University of Minnesota Press.

Fendrich, R., Wessinger, C.M., & Gazzaniga, M.S. (1992). Residual Vision in a Scotoma: Implications for Blindsight. *Science 258*, 1489-91.

Flanagan, O. (1992). *Consciousness Reconsidered*. Cambridge, MA: The MIT Press.

Fodor, J.A. (1968). *Psychological Explanation: An Introduction to the Philosophy of Psychology*. New York: Random House.

Fodor, J.A. (1974). Special Sciences. *Synthese 28*, 77-115.

Fodor, J.A. (1981). The Appeal to Tacit Knowledge in Psychological Explanations. In *Representations*. Cambridge: The MIT Press. 63-78.

Gazzaniga, M.S., Fendrich, R., & Wessinger, C.M. (1994). Blindsight Reconsidered. *Current Directions in Psychological Science 3* (3), 93-96.

Gettier, E.I. (1963). Is Justified True Belief Knowledge? *Analysis 23*, 121-123.

Gibson, J.J. (1979). *The Ecological Approach to Visual Perception*. Boston: Houghton Mifflin.

Goldman, A.I. (1967). A Causal Theory of Knowing. *Journal of Philosophy 64*(12), 355-72.

Goldman, A.I. (1976). Discrimination and Perceptual Knowledge. *Journal of Philosophy 73* (20), 771-91.

Goldman, A.I. (1979). Reliabilism: What Is Justified Belief? In G.S. Pappas (ed.). *Justification and Knowledge*. Dordrecht: D. Reidel. 1-23.

Goodale, M.A., & Humphrey, G.K. (1998). The Objects of Action and Perception. *Cognition 67*, 179-205.

Graves, R.E., & Jones, B.S. (1992). Conscious Visual Perceptual Awareness vs. Non-Conscious Visual Spatial Localization Examined with Normal Subjects Using Possible Analogues of Blindsight and Neglect. *Cognitive Neuropsychology 9*, 487-508.

Hardcastle, V.G. (1996). The Why of Consciousness: A Non-Issue for Materialists. *Journal of Consciousness Studies 3* (1), 7-13.

Heil, J. (1983). *Perception and Cognition*. Berkeley, CA: University of California Press.

Heywood, C.A., Cowey, A., & Newcombe, F. (1991). Chromatic Discrimination in a Cortically Colour Blind Observer. *Journal of Neuroscience* (Europe) 3, 902-12.

Holmes, G. (1918). Disturbances of Vision by Cerebral Lesions. *British Journal of Ophthalmology 2*, 353-84.

Holt, J. (1998). Blindsight: An Essay in the Philosophy of Psychology and Mind. Dissertation, University of Western Ontario.

Holt, J. (1999). Blindsight in Debates about Qualia. *Journal of Consciousness Studies 6* (5), 54-71.

Horgan, T. (1984). Jackson on Physical Information and Qualia. *Philosophical Quarterly 34*, 147-151.

Horst, S. (1995). Phenomenology and Psychophysics. Manuscript, Wesleyan University.

Humphrey, N. (1970). What the Frog's Eye Tells the Monkey's Brain. *Brain, Behavior, and Evolution 3*, 324-37.

Humphrey, N. (1974). Vision in a Monkey without Striate Cortex: A Case Study. *Perception 3*, 241-55.

Humphrey, N. (1992). *A History of the Mind*. New York: Simon & Schuster.

Jackson, F. (1982). Epiphenomenal Qualia. *Philosophical Quarterly 32*, 127-36.

Jackson, F. (1986). What Mary Didn't Know. *Journal of Philosophy 83*, 291-95.

Klüver, H. (1936). An Analysis of the Effects of the Removal of the Occipital Lobes in Monkeys. *Journal of Psychology 2*, 49-61.

Klüver, H. (1941). Visual Functions After the Removal of the Occipital Lobes. *Journal of Psychology 11*, 23-45.

Klüver, H. (1942). Functional Significance of the Geniculo-Striate System. *Biological Symposium 3*, 253-99.

Kolb, F.C., & Braun, J. (1995). Blindsight in Normal Observers. *Nature 337*, 336-38.

Kripke, S. (1972). *Naming and Necessity*. Cambridge, MA: Harvard University Press.

Landesman, C. (1993). Why Nothing Has Color: Color Skepticism. In Pojman, 121-26.

Lehrer, K. (1993). A Critique of Externalism. In Pojman, 306-19.

Levine, J. (1983). Materialism and Qualia: The Explanatory Gap. *Pacific Philosophical Quarterly 64*, 354-61.

Lewis, D. (1980). Mad Pain and Martian Pain. In N. Block (ed.). *Readings in Philosophy of Psychology*. 2 vols. Cambridge, MA: Harvard University Press. 216-22.

Loar, B. (1990). Phenomenal States. In J.E. Tomberlin (ed.). *Philosophical Perspectives 4: Action Theory and Philosophy of Mind*. Atascadero, CA: Ridgeview. 81-107.

Malcolm, N. (1952). Two Types of Knowledge. *Mind 51*, 178-89.

Marcel, A.J. (1983). Conscious and Unconscious Perception: An Approach to the Relations between Phenomenal Experience and Perceptual Processes. *Cognitive Psychology 15*, 238-300.

Marcel, A.J. (1988). Phenomenal Experience and Functionalism. In Marcel & Bisiach, 121-58.

Marcel, A.J. (1998). Blindsight and Shape Perception: Deficit of Visual Consciousness or of Visual Function? *Brain 121*, 1565-88.

Marcel, A.J., & Bisiach, E. (eds.) (1988). *Consciousness in Contemporary Science*. New York: Oxford University Press.

Marr, D. (1982). *Vision*. San Francisco, CA: Freeman.

Marras, A. (1993). Psychophysical Supervenience and Nonreductive Materialism. *Synthese 95*, 275-304.

Marras, A. (1994). Nonreductive Materialism and Mental Causation. *Canadian Journal of Philosophy 24*, 465-494.

Marshall, J. & Halligan, P. (1998). Blindsight and Insight into Visuo-Spatial Neglect. *Nature* (London) *336*, 766-77.

McCauley, R.N. (1993). Why the Blind Can't Lead the Blind: Dennett on the Blind Spot, Blindsight, and Sensory Qualia. *Consciousness and Cognition 2*, 155-64.

McGinn, C. (1991). *The Problem of Consciousness*. Oxford: Blackwell.

McGinn, C. (1997). *Minds and Bodies*. New York: Oxford University Press.

McLeod, P., Dittrich, W., Driver, J., Perret, D., & Zihl, J. (1996). Preserved and Impaired Detection of Structure from Motion by a Motion-Blind Patient. *Visual Cognition 3*, 363-91.

Mellor, H. (1977). Conscious Belief. *Proceedings of the Aristotelian Society 68*, 87-101.

Michel, F., & Peronnet, F. (1980). A Case of Cortical Deafness: Clinical and Electrophysiological Data. *Brain and Language 10*, 367-77.

Milner, A.D., & Goodale, M.A. (1995). *The Visual Brain in Action*. New York: Oxford University Press.

Moore, G.E. (1942). Reply to My Critics. In P. Schlipp (ed.), *The Philosophy of G.E. Moore*. La Salle, IL: Open Court. 535-677.

Nagel, T. (1971). Brain Bisection and the Unity of Consciousness. *Synthese 22*, 396-413.

Nagel, T. (1974). What Is It Like to Be a Bat? *Philosophical Review 83*, 435-50.

Nagel, T. (1986). *The View From Nowhere*. New York: Oxford.

Natsoulas, T. (1982). Conscious Perception and the Paradox of Blindsight. In G. Underwood (ed.). *Aspects of Consciousness*. New York: Academic Press. 79-109.

Natsoulas, T. (1997). Blindsight and Consciousness. *American Journal of Psychology 110*, 1-33.

Nelkin, N. (1994). Phenomena and Representation. *British Journal for the Philosophy of Science 45*, 527-47.

Nelkin, N. (1996). *Consciousness and the Origins of Thought*. Cambridge: Cambridge University Press.

Paillard, J., Michel, F., & Stelmach, G. (1983). Localization Without Content: A Tactile Analogue of Blindsight. *Archives of Neurology 40*, 548-51.

Parfit, D. (1984). *Reasons and Persons*. New York: Oxford University Press.

Penfield, W. (1958). *The Excitable Cortex in Conscious Man*. Liverpool: Liverpool University Press.

Penrose, R. (1989). *The Emperor's New Mind*. New York: Oxford University Press.

Pojman, L.P. (1993). *The Theory of Knowledge*. Belmont, CA: Wadsworth.

Pöppel, E., Held, R., & Frost, D. (1973). Residual Visual Function After Brain Wounds Involving the Central Visual Pathways in Man. *Nature* (London) *243*, 295-96.

Puccetti, R. (1973). Brain Bisection and Personal Identity. *British Journal for the Philosophy of Science 24*, 339-55.

Putnam, H. (1960). Minds and Machines. In S. Hook (ed.). *Dimensions of Mind*. New York: New York University Press. 148-79.

Pylyshyn, Z. (1999). Is Vision Continuous with Cognition? The Case for Cognitive Impenetrability of Visual Perception. *Behavioral and Brain Sciences 22* (3), 341-423.

Ramachandran, V.S., & Gregory, R.L. (1991). Perceptual Filling In of Artificially Induced Scotomas in Human Vision. *Nature 350*, 699-702.

Raymont, P. (1995). Tye's Criticism of the Knowledge Argument. *Dialogue 34*, 713-26.

Reingold, E.M., & Merikle, P.M. (1993). Theory and Measurement in the Study of Unconscious Processes. In M. Davies & G.W. Humphreys (eds.). *Consciousness: Psychological and Philosophical Essays.* Oxford: Blackwell. 40-57.

Riddoch, G. (1917). Dissociation of Visual Perceptions Due to Occipital Injuries, with Especial Reference to Appreciation of Movement. *Brain 40*, 15-57.

Rossetti, Y., Rode, G., & Boisson, D. (1995). Implicit Processing of Somaesthetic Information: A Dissociation Between Where and How? *NeuroReport 6*, 506-10.

Russell, B. (1910-1911). Knowledge by Acquaintance and Knowledge by Description. *Proceedings of the Aristotelian Society 11*, 108-28.

Ryle, G. (1949). *The Concept of Mind.* London: Hutchinson.

Sanders, M.D., Warrington, E.K., Marshall, J., & Weiskrantz, L. (1974). "Blindsight": Vision in a Field Defect. *Lancet 5* (20), 707-08.

Searle, J.R. (1983). *Intentionality: An Essay in the Philosophy of Mind.* Cambridge: Cambridge University Press.

Searle, J.R. (1984). *Minds, Brains, and Science.* Cambridge, MA: Harvard University Press.

Shallice, T. (1988). Information-Processing Models of Consciousness. In Marcel & Bisiach, 305-33.

Siewert, C. (1998). *The Significance of Consciousness.* Princeton, NJ: Princeton University Press.

Sperry, R. (1974). Lateral Specialization in the Surgically Separated Hemispheres. In F. O. Schmitt & F.G. Worden (eds.). *The Neurosciences: Third Study Program.* Cambridge, MA: The MIT Press.

Stoerig, P. (1998). Wavelength Information Processing Versus Color Perception: Evidence from Blindsight and Color-Blindsight. In W.G.K. Backhaus, R. Kliegl & J.S. Werner (eds.). *Color Vision: Perspectives from Different Disciplines.* New York: Walter de Gruyter.

Stoerig, P., & Cowey, A. (1997). Blindsight in Man and Monkey. *Brain 120*, 552-59.

Tranel, D., & Damasio, A. (1985). Knowledge Without Awareness: An Autonomic Index of Facial Recognition by Prosopagnosics. *Science 228*, 1453-55.

Tye, M. (1989). *The Metaphysics of Mind*. Cambridge: Cambridge University Press.

Tye, M. (1993). Blindsight, the Absent Qualia Hypothesis, and the Mystery of Consciousness. In C. Hookway & D. Peterson (eds.). *Philosophy and Cognitive Science: Royal Institute of Philosophy Supplement 34*, 19-40.

Tye, M. (1995). *Ten Problems of Consciousness: A Representational Theory of the Phenomenal Mind*. Cambridge, MA: The MIT Press.

Vaina, L.M. (1995). Akinetopsia, Achromatopsia, and Blindsight: Recent Studies on Perception without Awareness. *Synthese 105*, 253-71.

Velmans, M. (1991). Is Human Information Processing Conscious? *Behavioral and Brain Sciences 14*, 651-726.

Vision, G. (1997). *Problems of Vision*. New York: Oxford University Press.

Vision, G. (1998). Blindsight and Philosophy. *Philosophical Psychology 11*, 137-59.

Weiskrantz, L. (1986). *Blindsight: A Case Study and Implications*. Oxford: Clarendon.

Weiskrantz, L. (1995). Blindsight—Not an Island Unto Itself. *Current Directions in Psychological Science 4* (5), 146-49.

Weiskrantz, L. (1997). *Consciousness Lost and Found*. New York: Oxford University Press.

Weiskrantz, L., Warrington, E.K., Sanders, M.D., & Marshall, J. (1974). Visual Capacity in the Hemianopic Field Following a Restricted Occipital Ablation. *Brain 97*, 709-28.

Weiskrantz, L., Barbur, J., & Sahraie, A. (1995). Parameters Affecting Conscious Versus Unconscious Discrimination with Damage to the Visual Cortex (V1). *Proceedings of the National Academy of Science 92*, 6122-26.

Werth, R. (1983). Blindsight: Some Conceptual Considerations. *Behavioral and Brain Sciences 3*, 467-68.

Wilson, M. (1985). What Is This Thing Called Pain? The Philosophy of Science Behind the Contemporary Debate. *Pacific Philosophical Quarterly 66*, 227-67.

Zihl, J., von Cramon, D., & Mai, N. (1983). Selective Disturbance of Movement Vision After Bilateral Brain Damage. *Brain 106*, 313-40.